Please

3o~minute crochet

30~minute crochet

what can you crochet in half an hour or less?

carol meldrum

Search Press

This edition published in 2013 by
Search Press Ltd
Wellwood
North Farm Road
Tunbridge Wells
Kent TN2 3DR

A Quintet Book

ISBN-13: 978-1-84448-968-8

This book was designed and produced by
Quintet Publishing Limited, 6 Blundell Street,
London N7 9BH, UK

Project Editor: Caroline Elliker
Designer: Tania Field
Photographer: Sussie Bell
Illustrator: Veronica Wood
Art Director: Michael Charles
Managing Editor: Emma Bastow
Publisher: Mark Searle

Printed in China by 1010 Printing Group Limited

9 8 7 6 5 4 3 2 1

This book contains material used in previous publications.

contents

introduction

Think you're too busy to crochet anything? Think again! Here's a collection of crochet projects that you really can fit into your spare time. Be inspired to pick up your hook and yarn, dip into this fantastic book and get crocheting.

Each pattern has been designed so you will see results fast, and they can easily be worked from those little scraps of yarn left over from other projects. You will be surprised at just how much you can create in those half-hour pockets of time scattered throughout the day!

The book includes full instructions covering all the techniques used in the patterns, so it's a perfect place to start if you are new to crochet and looking to expand your skills. For the more experienced there is a mix of slightly more advanced techniques to keep you interested throughout. Projects are labelled 'beginner', 'intermediate' or 'advanced' to help you select those most suited to your skills and ability, and there is a useful reference section at the end containing diagrams and step-by-step techniques.

With such a wide variety of projects at your fingertips, you will keep coming back to this collection. Whether it's for last-minute gift ideas or simply just an urge to craft and create, there is something here for everyone.

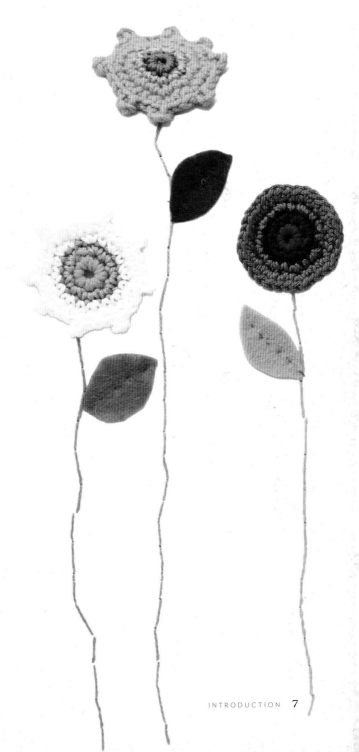

30~minute projects

wild strawberry
page 11

toadstool
page 12

acorn
page 15

leaf motifs
page 16

tree decoration
page 18

butterfly
page 21

finger puppets
page 22

birdie
page 26

owl
page 27

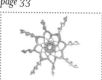

hedgehog
page 28

mouse pincushion
page 29

owl mask
page 30

animal ears
page 32

snowflake
page 33

cup cosy
page 35

container with handle
page 36

glass stem marker
page 37

snug coaster
page 38

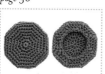

plant pot
page 39

string bag bottle holder
page 40

napkin rings
page 41

fancy jam jar cover
page 42

place mat
page 44

circle to square coaster
page 45

granny square table
runner *page 46*

stacking pots
page 48

bunny egg cosy
page 51

owl egg cosy
page 52

trivet
page 53

heart motif bag
page 55

large heart neck purse
page 56

rolled wrist band
page 57

lipstick case
page 58

flower key chain
page 59

hexagon motif purse
page 60

layered picot necklace
page 61

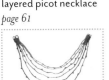

layered circular motif cushion *page 62*

granny square slip cover *page 64*

floral cushion motifs
page 66

picture frame
page 69

covered coat hanger
page 70

card pouch
page 71

luggage tag
page 72

chalk bag
page 73

basic phone case
page 74

advanced phone case
page 75

crochet cushion trim
page 76

earrings
page 79

covered buttons
page 80

zombie pin badge
page 82

glasses chain
page 83

bow tie
page 85

hair bow
page 86

flower headband
page 87

bracelet
page 88

lace motif on purse
page 89

lace necklace
page 90

peter pan collar
page 91

layered brooch
page 93

scarf
page 94

cloche hat
page 95

belt
page 96

ring
page 97

BEGINNER

INTERMEDIATE

EXPERIENCED

wild strawberry

This strawberry-inspired project is created using a mixture of increasing and decreasing techniques, with a touch of embroidery around the outside for the seeds. They make the perfect summertime table decoration.

INTERMEDIATE

MATERIALS
Rowan Cotton Glacé (100% cotton; approx. 115m/125yd per 50g/1¾oz ball)

A shade 741 Poppy x 1 ball

B shade 739 Dijon x 1 ball

C shade 856 Mineral x 1 ball for embroidery

EQUIPMENT
Crochet hook size 3mm (US D/3)

Embroidery needle

Toy stuffing

GAUGE
25 sts x 25 rows = 10cm (4in) in double crochet

FINISHED SIZE
Length 6cm (2¼in), circumference 10cm (4in)

◄ projects

PATTERN

strawberry

Using yarn A and 3mm (US D/3) hook, ch2.

Round 1: 6dc into 2nd ch from hook, sl st into ch1 at beg of round. (6 sts)

Round 2: Ch1, 1dc into each st to end, sl st into ch1 at beg of round.

Round 3: Ch1, 1dc into 1st st, * 2dc into next st, 1dc into next st, rep from * to last st, 2dc into last st, sl st into ch1 at beg of round. (9 sts)

Round 4: Ch1, 1dc into 1st 2 sts, * 2dc into next st, 1dc into next 2 sts, rep from * to last st, 2dc into last st, sl st into ch1 at beg of round. (12 sts)

Round 5: Ch1, 1dc into 1st 3 sts, * 2dc into next st, 1dc into next 3 sts, rep from * to last st, 2dc into last st, sl st into ch1 at beg of round. (15 sts)

Round 6: Ch1, 1dc into 1st 4 sts, * 2dc into next st, 1dc into next 4 sts, rep from * to last st, 2dc into last st, sl st into ch1 at beg of round. (18 sts)

Round 7: Ch1, 1dc into 1st 5sts, * 2dc into next st, 1dc into next 5 sts, rep from * to last st, 2dc into last st, sl st into ch1 at beg of round. (21 sts)

Round 8: Ch1, 1dc into each st to end, sl st into ch1 at beg of round.

Round 9: Ch1, 1dc into 1st 6 sts, * 2dc into next st, 1dc into next 6 sts, rep from * to last st, 2dc into last st, sl st into ch1 at beg of round. (24 sts)

Rounds 10 – 11: As round 8.

Round 12: ch1, 1dc into 1st 2 sts, * 2dctog over next 2 sts, 1dc into next 2 sts, rep from * until last 2 sts, 2dctog over last 2 sts, sl st into ch1 at beg of round. (18 sts)

Round 13: ch1, 1dc into 1st st, * 2dctog over next 2 sts, 1dc into next st, rep from * until last 2 sts, 2dctog over last 2 sts, sl st into ch1 at beg of round. (12 sts)

Insert stuffing.

Round 14: Ch1, 2dctog over 1st 2 sts, * 2dctog over next 2 sts, rep from * to end sl st into ch1 at beg of round. (6 sts)

Fasten off yarn leaving long enough length to sew up top opening.

LEAF TOP

Using yarn B and 3mm (US D/3) hook, ch6 + 1ch.

Row 1: * 1dc into 2nd ch from hook, 1htr into next ch, 1dc into next ch, 1htr into next ch, 1dc into next ch, sl st into last ch, ch 7, rep from * 4 more times.

Fasten off yarn.

ASSEMBLY

Sew up top opening of strawberry and stitch leaf to top of strawberry.

Weave in loose ends.

Using yarn C and picture as guide work French Knots around the body of the strawberry.

toadstool

Mark the turning of the seasons with this crochet toadstool. The stem and top are worked separately then stitched into place. The top is made up of classic red with white felt spots, which are appliquéd randomly over the surface.

MATERIALS

Rowan Cotton Glacé
(100% cotton; approx.
115m/125yd per 50g/
1¾oz ball)

A shade 726 Bleached x 1

B shade 741 Poppy x 1

White felt for spots

White sewing cotton thread

Polyester toy stuffing

EQUIPMENT

Crochet hook size 3mm
(US D/3)

Sharp sewing needle

Sewing up needle

GAUGE

Not crucial

FINISHED SIZE

Approx. 7cm (2¾in)
high, 4.5cm (1¾in) wide

PATTERN

stalk

Using yarn A and 3mm (US D/3) hook, ch2.

Round 1: Work 8dc into 2nd ch from hook, sl st into ch1 at beg of round. (8 sts)

Round 2: Ch1, 2dc into each st to end, sl st into ch1 at beg of round. (16 sts)

Round 3: Ch1, 1dc into back loop of each st to end, sl st into ch1 at beg of round.

Round 4: Ch1, 1dc into 1st 2 sts, * 2dctog over next 2 sts, 1dc into next 2 sts, rep from * to last 2 sts, 2dctog over last 2 sts, sl st into ch1 at beg of round. (12 sts)

Round 5: Ch1, 1dc into each st to end, sl st into ch1 at beg of round.

Round 6: Ch1, 1dc into 1st st, * 2dctog over next 2 sts, 1dc into next st, rep from * to last 2 sts, 2dctog over last 2 sts, sl st into ch1 at beg of round. (8 sts)

Rounds 7 – 10: As round 5.

Insert stuffing.

Fasten off yarn leaving a tail to sew up opening.

top

Using yarn B and 3mm (US D/3) hook, ch2.

Round 1: 6dc into 2nd ch from hook, sl st into ch1 at beg of round. (6 sts)

Round 2: Ch1, 1dc into 1st st, * 2dc into next st, 1dc into next st, rep from * to last st, 2dc into last st, sl st into ch1 at beg of round. (9 sts)

Round 3: Ch1, 1dc into each st to end, sl st into ch1 at beg of round.

Round 4: Ch1, 1dc into 1st 2 sts, * 2dc into next st, 1dc into next 2 sts, rep from * to last st, 2dc into last st, sl st into ch1 at beg of round. (12 sts)

Round 5: As round 3.

Round 6: Ch1, 1dc into 1st 3 sts, * 2dc into next st, 1dc into next 3 sts, rep from * to last st, 2dc into last st, sl st into ch1 at beg of round. (15 sts)

Round 7: Ch1, 1dc into 1st 4 sts, * 2dc into next st, 1dc into next 4 sts, rep from * to last st, 2dc into last st, sl st into ch1 at beg of round. (18 sts)

Round 8: Ch1, 1dc into 1st 5 sts, *2dc into next st, 1dc into next 5 sts, rep from * to last st, 2dc into last st, sl st into ch1 at beg of round. (21 sts)

Round 9: Ch1, 1dc into 1st 6 sts, * 2dc into next st, 1dc into next 6 sts, rep from * to last st, 2dc into last st, sl st into Ch1 at beg of round. (24 sts)

Fasten off yarn B and join in yarn A.

Round 10: Ch1, 1dc into back loop of

each st to end, sl st into ch1 at beg
of round.

Round 11: Ch1, 1dc into 1st 2 sts,
*2dctog over next 2 sts, 1dc into
next 2 sts, rep from * until last 2
sts, 2dctog over last 2 sts, sl st into
ch1 at beg of round. (18 sts)

Insert stuffing.

Round 12: Ch1, 1dc into 1st st,
*2dctog over next 2 sts, 1dc into
next st, rep from * until last 2 sts,
2dctog over last 2 sts, sl st into ch1
at beg of round. (12 sts)

Round 13: Ch1, 2dctog over 1st 2 sts,
* 2dctog over next 2 sts, rep from
* to end.

Fasten off yarn leaving long enough
length to sew up opening

ASSEMBLY

Sew up openings for top and bottom
sections, place top sections at
the centre of the stalk and stitch
into place.

FINISHING

Cut a selection of small circle sizes
from white felt and stitch into place
on the top section of toadstool.

acorn

Bring a piece of autumn into your home with this acorn design. The pattern is crocheted in the round, working into the back loop of the stitches to add a touch of texture. Basic increasing and decreasing techniques create the classic acorn shape.

MATERIALS

Rowan Felted Tweed DK (50% merino, 25% alpaca, 25% viscose; approx. 175m/191yd per 50g/ 1¾oz ball)

A shade 161 Avocado x 1 ball

B shade 177 Clay x 1 ball

C shade 157 Camel x 1 ball

D shade 145 Treacle x 1 ball

Acorn 1 – yarn A & B

Acorn 2 – yarn C & D

Acorn 3 – yarn D & A

Polyester toy stuffing

EQUIPMENT

Crochet hook size 3mm (US D/3)

GAUGE

Not crucial

FINISHED SIZE

Approx. 4cm (1½in)

PATTERN

Using yarn A and 3mm (US D/3) hook ch2.

Round 1: Work 6dc into 2nd ch from hook, sl st into ch1 at beg of round. (6 sts)

Work next 3 rounds as follows working into the back loop of each st:

Round 2: Ch1, * 1dc into 1st st, 2dc into next st, 1dc into next st, rep from * to last st, 2dc into last st, sl st into ch1 at beg of round. (9 sts)

Rounds 3–4: Ch1, 1dc into each st to end, sl st into ch1 at beg of round.

Break off yarn A and join in yarn B.

Round 5: Ch1, 2dc into 1st st, 2dc into each st to end, sl st into ch1 at beg of round. (18 sts)

Round 6: Working into the back loop of all sts, ch1, 1dc into each st to end, sl st into ch1 at beg of round.

Round 7: Ch1, 1dc into next 4 sts, * 2dctog over next 2 sts, 1dc into next 4 sts, rep from * once more, 2dctog over last 2 sts, sl st into ch1 at beg of round. (15 sts)

Round 8: Ch1, 1dc into next 3 sts, *2dctog over next 2 sts, 1dc into next 4 sts, rep from * once more, 2dctog over last 2 sts, sl st into ch1 at beg of round. (12 sts)

Insert stuffing.

Round 9: Ch1, 2dctog over 1st 2 sts, *2dctog over next 2 sts, rep from * to end, sl st into ch1 at beg of round.

stalk

Work 1sl st to close top opening, then ch5, 1dc into 2nd ch from hook, 1dc into next ch3, sl st back into base of stalk.

Fasten off yarn leaving long enough tail to finish sewing up top opening.

FINISHING

Weave in ends.

leaf motifs

These leaf shapes make fun and versatile motifs. Stitch them onto fabric, or add to a flower design, for a finishing touch. They are good next-step projects for beginners and the more adventurous can easily adapt them to make other leaf shapes.

PATTERN

Using colour of choice and 3mm (US D/3) hook, ch18 + 1 turning chain.

Row 1: 1dc into 2nd ch from hook, 1htr into next 7ch, 1dc into next ch, 1sl st into next ch, ch12, 1dc into 2nd ch from hook, 1htr into next 6ch, 1dc into next ch, 1sl st into next ch, ch11, 1dc into 2nd ch from hook, 1htr into next 5ch, 1dc into next ch, 1sl st into next ch, ch10, 1dc into 2nd ch from hook, 1htr into next 4ch, 1dc into next ch, 1sl st into next ch, (ch7, 1dc into 2nd ch from hook, 1htr into next 4ch, 1dc into next ch, 1sl st into same ch as last sl st) twice, work back down the stem securing each leaf into base of matching leaf on the opposite side as follows, sl st into next ch2, ch8, 1dc into 2nd ch from hook, 1htr into next 5ch, 1dc into next ch, sl st into base of leaf, sl st into next ch2, ch9, 1dc into 2nd ch from hook, 1htr into next 6ch, 1dc into next ch, sl st into base of leaf, sl st into next ch2, ch10, 1dc into 2nd ch from hook, 1htr into next 7ch, 1dc into next ch, sl st into base of leaf , sl st into last 8ch and fasten off.

FINISHING

Weave in loose ends, then block and press gently.

MATERIALS

Rowan Cotton Glacé (100% cotton; approx. 115m/125yd per 50g/1¾oz ball)

A shade 856 Mineral x 1 ball

B shade 837 Baked Red x 1 ball

EQUIPMENT

Crochet hook size 3mm (US D/3)

GAUGE

Not crucial

FINISHED SIZE

Approx. 6.5cm x 11.5cm (2½in x 4½in)

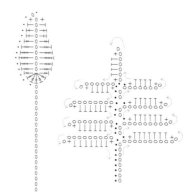

SEE DIAGRAMS PAGE 120

MATERIALS

Rowan Cotton Glacé (100% cotton; approx. 115m/125yd per 50g/1¾oz ball), shade 739 Dijon x 1 ball

EQUIPMENT

Crochet hook size 3mm (US D/3)

GAUGE

Not crucial

FINISHED SIZE

Approx. 3.5cm x 6cm (1¼ in x 2¼ in), length of tail 6cm (2¼in)

SPECIAL ABBREVIATIONS

Linked stitches: The stems of all the basic stitches, except for double crochet, can be linked to each other in the middle. Instead of wrapping the yarn around the hook to achieve the length of stitch, insert the hook down through the horizontal loops around the stem of the stitch, then wrap the yarn around the hook and draw through. Once the required number of loops have been achieved, insert the hook into the stitch and complete as you would normally.

Ldc – linked double crochet

Ltr – linked treble crochet

Ldtr – linked double treble

Lttr – linked triple treble

LQuadtr – linked quadruple treble

PATTERN

Using yarn and 3mm (US D/3) hook, ch10 + 1 turning chain.

Row 1: 1dc into 2nd ch from hook, 1htr into next ch, 1(Ldc) linked double crochet into next 2ch, 1Ltr into next ch, 1Ldtr into next ch, 1Lttr into next ch, 1LQuadtr, 1Ldtr into next ch, 1Ltr into next ch, 7Ltr into last chain.

Work back along the underside of chain as follows: 1Ltr into next ch, 1Lttr into next ch, 1Ldtr into next ch, 1LQuadtr into next ch, 1Lttr into next ch, 1Dtr into next ch, 1Ltr into next ch, 1Ldc into next 2ch, 1htr into next ch, 1dc into last ch.

Work 1sl st into top of next 13 sts, ch20.

Fasten off yarn.

FINISHING

Weave in loose ends, then block and press gently.

tree decoration

Make a scene with this crochet tree design! The project is made up of two identical panels, worked from a centre chain to the outer edge, playing with different stitches to create the tree shape.

PATTERN
(MAKE FRONT AND BACK ALIKE)

Using yarn A and 3mm (US D/3) hook, ch15 + 1 turning chain.

Row 1: 1dc into 2nd ch from hook, 1dc into next ch14, 3dc into last ch, work back down underside of chain, 1dc into each ch to end, turn. (31 sts)

Row 2: Ch1, 1dc into 1st st, 1dc into next 15 sts, 3dc into next st, 1dc into each st to end, turn. (33 sts)

Row 3: Ch3, 2dc into 1st st, 1dc into next 4 sts, 1htr into next 5 sts, 1dc into next 6 sts, (1htr, 1dc, 1htr) into next st, 1dc into next 6 sts, 1htr into next 5 sts, 1dc into next 4 sts, 1dc into last st, turn. (37 sts)

Row 4: Ch3, 2dc into 1st st, 1dc into next 2 sts, 1htr into next 2 sts, 1dc into next st, sl st into next st, ch3, work 2dc into same sp as sl st just worked, 1dc into next st, 1htr into next 2 sts, 1dc into next st, sl st into next st, ch3, work 2dc into same sp as sl st just worked, * 1dc into next st, 1htr into next 2 sts, 1dc into next 3 sts, (1htr, 1dc, 1htr) into next st, 1dc into next 3 sts, 1htr into next 2 sts, 1dc into next st, 2dc into next st, ch3, sl st into same st as last dc, rep from * once more, 1dc into next st, 1htr into next 2 sts, 1dc into next st, 1dc into last st, turn. (45 sts)

Row 5: Ch3, 2dc into 1st st, 1dc into next st, 1htr into next st, 1dc into next 3 sts, sl st into next st and base of dc from prev row, work 3sl st up ch3 and into top of dc from prev round, ch2, 2htr into same st, 1htr into next st, 1dc into next st, sl st into next 3 sts, sl st into base of dc from prev row, work 3sl st up ch3 and into top of next st, ch1, 2dc into same st, 1dc into next st, sl st into next 6 sts, work (1dc, 1htr, 1dc) into next st, sl st into next 6 sts, 1dc into next st, 2dc into next st, ch1, sl st into base of st just worked, sl st down ch3, sl st into base of dc from prev round, 1sl st into next 4 sts, 1dc into next st, 1htr into next st, 2htr into next st, ch2, sl st into base of stitch just worked, sl st down ch3, sl st into base of dc from prev row, sl st into next 3 sts, 1dc into next st, 1htr into next st, 1dc into next st, 2dc into last st.

Fasten off yarn.

MATERIALS

Rowan Felted Tweed DK (50% merino, 25% alpaca, 25% viscose; approx. 175m/191yd per 50g/ 1¾oz ball)

A shade 158 Pine x 1 ball

B shade 161 Avocado x 1 ball

Medium florist wire, approx. 30cm (12in) length

Wine cork

EQUIPMENT

Crochet hook size 3mm (US D/3)

GAUGE

Not crucial

FINISHED SIZE

Approx. 12.5cm (5in) deep, 9cm (3½in) wide

ASSEMBLY

Block and press front and back
    panels, stretching out the peaks
    to help define tree shape.

With wrong sides together, sew
    around the outer edge of the tree
    leaving the bottom open.

Bend the florist wire in half and
    insert in between the front and
    back panels. Stitch into place using
    matching yarn.

Place the ends of the wire into the
    cork to allow the tree to stand free.

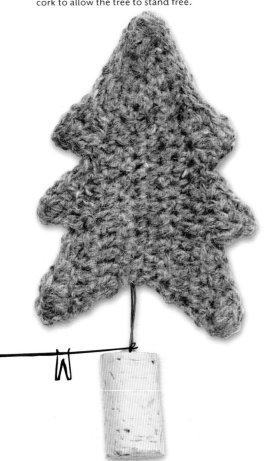

butterfly

This little butterfly design is worked in one piece. The wings are created by changing the length of the stitch and defined by their changing colour, while the beaded body adds a touch of sparkle. This project can be easily adapted into a brooch or hair clip.

MATERIALS

Brown Sheep Nature Spun Worsted (100% wool; approx. 224m/245yd per 100g/3½oz ball)

A shade 052 French Clay x 1 ball

B shade 047 Peruvian Pink x 1 ball

Beads: 1 black seed bead, 2 yellow seed beads, 5 black 6mm (⅓in) beads

Craft wire

EQUIPMENT

Crochet hook size 3mm (US D/3)

GAUGE

Not crucial

FINISHED SIZE

Approx. 7cm x 5.5cm (2¾ in x 2 in)

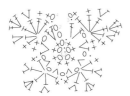

SEE DIAGRAM PAGE 121

◄ projects

PATTERN

Using yarn A and 3mm (US D/3) hook, ch4, join ends together with sl st to form a ring.

Round 1: Ch1, 8dc into ring, join with sl st into ch1 at beg of round. (8 sts)

Round 2: Ch2, 2dc into 1st st, ch1, 2htr into next st, ch1, (2dc into next st, 1ch) 4 times, 2htr into next st, ch1, 2dc into last st, turn.

Next Row: Miss 2 sts, (4dc, 2htr, 1dc) into next 1ch sp, miss 2 sts, sl st into next ch1 sp, (miss 2 sts, 5htr into next ch1sp, miss 2 sts, sl st into next ch1sp) twice, miss 2 sts, (1dc, 2htr, 4dc) into next ch1sp, miss 2 sts, sl st into top of ch2 from prev row, turn.

Break off yarn A and join in yarn B.

Next Row: Ch1, 1dc into next 2 sts, 2htr into next st, 3dc into next st, 2htr into next st, 1dc into next 2 sts, (miss next sl st, 1dc into next st, 2htr into next st, 3htr into next st, 2htr into next st, 1dc into next st) twice, miss next sl st, 1dc into next 2 sts, 2htr into next st, 3dc into next st, 2htr into next st, 1dc into next 2 sts.

FINISHING

Weave in loose ends, gently block and press into shape.

ASSEMBLY

beaded body

Cut a 30cm (12in) length of craft wire and thread black seed bead onto wire and place at the centre.

Fold the wire in half and gently twirl the bead with your fingers; this will twist the wire and secure the position of the bead, ensuring that the others stay in position.

Slip five 6mm (⅓ in) round black beads onto both sections of wire.

Make the antenna by slipping a yellow seed bead onto 1 end of wire, slide down towards the head, leaving approx. 2.5cm (1in), then fold wire in half and twist to make antenna. Repeat for the other end.

Thread the ends of wire back down through top circular bead and wrap around the base to secure. Repeat this process for remaining antenna.

Using picture as a guide, place body on crochet butterfly wings section and sew into place using either craft wire or thread.

finger puppets

These finger puppets are fun to create. The designs are worked in a similar way and given their own personality by adding different features. Why not mix it up to create your own wild things!

miss kitty

PATTERN

body

Using yarn A and 3mm (US D/3) hook, ch4, sl st to form ring.

Round 1: Ch1, 6dc into ring, sl st into ch1 at beg of round. (6 sts)

Round 2: Ch1, 2dc into 1st st, 2dc into each st to end, sl st into ch1 at beg of round. (12 sts)

Rounds 3 – 10: Ch1, 1dc into each st, sl st into ch1 at beg of round.

Fasten off.

head

Using yarn B and D/3 hook, ch4, sl st to form ring.

Round 1: Ch1, 6dc into ring, sl st into ch1 at beg of round. (6 sts)

Round 2: Ch1, 2dc into 1st 3 sts, 1dc into each st to end, sl st into ch1 at beg of round. (9 sts)

Fasten off yarn B and join in yarn A.

Round 3: Ch1, 1dc into 1st st, (2dc into next st, 1dc into next st) twice, 2dc into next st, 1dc into last 3 sts, sl st into ch1 at beg of round. (12 sts)

Round 4: Ch1, 1dc into each st.

Round 5: Ch1, 1dc into 1st 2 sts, (2dc into next st, 1dc into next 2 sts) twice, 2dc into next st, 1dc into last 3 sts, sl st into ch1 at beg of round. (15 sts)

Round 6: As round 4.

Round 7: Ch1, 1dc into 1st 3 sts, (2dc into next st, 1dc into next 3 sts) twice, 2dc into next st, 1dc into last 3 sts, sl st into ch1 at beg of round. (18 sts)

Round 8: Ch1, 1dc into 1st st, 1dc into each st to end, sl st into ch1 at beg of round.

Round 9: Ch1, 1dc into 1st st, * 2dctog over next 2 sts, 1dc into next st, rep from * until last 2 sts, 2dctog over last 2 sts, sl st into ch1 at beg of round. (12 sts)

Insert stuffing.

Round 10: Ch1, 2dctog over 1st 2 sts, * 2dctog over next 2 sts, rep from * to end, sl st into ch1 at beg of round. (6 sts)

MATERIALS

Rowan Felted Tweed DK (50% merino wool, 25% alpaca, 25% viscose; approx. 175m/191yd per 50g/1¾oz ball)

A shade 159 Carbon x 1 ball

B shade 177 Clay x 1 ball

Small amount of toy stuffing for head

Black and pink embroidery thread

Craft wire for tail

Green buttons x 2 for eyes

EQUIPMENT

Crochet hook size 3mm (US D/3)

Sewing up needle

GAUGE

Approx. 30 sts x 25 rows = 4 in (10cm) in double crochet

FINISHED SIZE

Approx. 7cm (2¾in)

Break off yarn leaving a long tail to
close opening at the back
of head.

ears (make 2)

Using yarn A and D/3 hook, ch3.

Row 1: (2htr, 1dc, 2htr) into 3rd
ch from hook.

Fasten off yarn.

tail

Using yarn B and D/3 hook, ch2.

Row 1: 4dc into 2nd ch from hook,
turn. (4 sts)

Row 2: Ch1, 1dc into each st to
end, turn.

Rows 3–4: As row 2.

Break off yarn B and join in yarn A.

Work a further 14 rows in dc.

ASSEMBLY

Using picture as guide, sew the head
onto the top of the body, then sew
ears into position on head.

Cut a piece of wire approx. twice the
length of the tail and bend it so it is
slightly shorter than the tail, making

sure that the sharp ends are folded
into the centre.

Insert the wire into the tail and sew
down the side seam and bottom
opening to enclose the wire.

Sew the tail to the back of the body
with the contrast tipping to the top.
Bend into suitable shape and make
sure the ends of the wire do not
poke out.

FINISHING

Embroider facial features as follows:
Work the triangular nose to the
very front using pink embroidery
thread and satin stitch, then work
an upside down Y-shape
for mouth.

Sew buttons for eyes onto the face
and sew whiskers through the nose
using black embroidery thread.

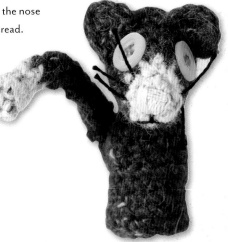

mr bear

PATTERN

body

Using 3mm (US D/3) hook and yarn A, ch4, sl st to form ring.

Round 1: ch1, 6dc into ring, sl st into ch1 at beg of round.

Round 2: ch1, 2dc into 1st st, 2dc into each st to end, sl st into ch1 at beg of round. (12sts)

Rounds 3–10: ch1, 1dc into each st, sl st into ch1 at beg of round.

head

Using 3mm (US D/3) hook and yarn B, ch4, sl st to form ring.

Round 1: ch1, 6dc into ring, sl st into ch1 at beg of round.

Fasten off yarn B and join in yarn A

Round 2: ch1, 2dc into 1st 3sts, 1dc into each st to end, sl st into ch1 at beg of round. (9sts)

Round 3: ch1, 1dc into 1st st, work (2dc into next st, 1dc into next st) twice, 2dc into next st , 1dc into last 3sts, sl st into ch1 at beg of round. (12sts)

Round 4: ch1, 1dc into each st.

Round 5: ch1, 1dc into 1st 2sts, work (2dc into next st, 1dc into next 2sts) twice, 2dc into next st, 1dc into last 3sts, sl st into ch1 at beg of round. (15sts)

Round 7: ch1, 1dc into 1st 3sts, work (2dc into next st, 1dc into next 3sts) twice, 2dc into next st, 1dc into last 3sts, sl st into ch1 at beg of round. (18sts)

Rounds 8 – 9: ch1, 1dc into 1st st, 1dc into each st to end, sl st into ch1 at beg of round.

Round 10: ch1, 1dc into 1st st, *2dctog over next 2sts, 1dc into next st, rep from * until last 2sts, 2dctog over last 2sts, sl st into ch1 at beg or round. (12sts)

Insert stuffing.

Round 13: ch1, 2dctog over 1st 2sts, * 2dctog over next 2sts, rep from * to end, sl st into ch1 at beg of round. (6sts)

Break off yarn leaving long length, use this length to close opening at the back of head.

ears (make 2)

Using 3mm (US D/3) hook and yarn A, ch2.

Row 1: work (1dc, 1htr, 1dc, 1htr, 1dc) into 2nd ch from hook.

Fasten off yarn.

arms (make 2)

Using 3mm (US D/3) hook and yarn B, ch2.

MATERIALS

Rowan Felted Tweed DK (50% merino wool, 25% alpaca, 25% vidcose; approx. 175m/191yd per 50g/1¾oz ball)

A shade 160 Gilt x 1 ball

B shade 177 Clay x 1 ball

Small amount of toy stuffing for head

Black and brown embroidery thread

EQUIPMENT

Crochet hook size 3mm (US D/3)

Sewing up needle

FINISHED SIZE:

Approx. 7cm (2¾in)

Row 1: 4dc into 2nd ch from
hook, turn.
Row 2: ch1, 1dc into each st to end.
Break off yarn B and join in yarn A.
Repeat last row 5 more times.
Next row: ch1, 1dc into 1st st, 2dctog
over next 2sts, 1dc into last st,
turn. (3sts)
Next row: ch1, 3dctog over 3sts.
Fasten off yarn leaving long enough
length to sew down back seam.

ASSEMBLY

Using picture as guide, sew the head
onto the top of the body, then sew
ears into position on head.
Sew up the back of the arms, then pin
and stitch onto the body.

FINISHING

Next embroider facial features
to bear.
First work the triangular nose shape
to the very front using brown
embroidery thread and satin stitch,
then work an upside down Y shape
for mouth.
Next attach the eyes using black
embroidery thread and French knot
stitch, wrapping the thread around
needle approx. 4 times.

birdie

This design is so sweet and a great way to understand how to create shapes when working in the round. It's perfect for using up all those bits of leftover yarn from other projects. Then raid the button jar for the perfect match!

PATTERN

front

Using yarn A and 2.5mm (US B/1) hook, ch2.

Round 1: 8dc into 2nd ch from hook, sl st into ch1 at beg of round. (8 sts)

Round 2: Ch1, 2dc into 1st st, 2dc into each st to end, sl st into ch1 at beg of round. (16 sts)

Round 3: Ch1, 1dc into 1st st, * 2dc into next st, 1dc into next st, rep from * to last st, 2dc into last st, sl st into ch1 at beg of round.

Work tail and head as follows:

Round 4: Ch6, 1dc into 2nd ch from hook, htr into next ch, 1dc into next ch, 1tr into each of the next 2ch, miss 4 sts, sl st into next st, 1 sl st into next 3 sts, miss 2 sts, 7dc into next st, miss 2 sts, sl st into each st to end, sl st into ch1 as base of tail.

Break off yarn.

back

Work rounds 1–3 as given for Front. Work head and tail as follows:

Round 4: Sl st into 1st 10 sts, miss 2 sts, 7dc into next st, miss 2 sts, 1sl st into next 4 sts, make ch6, 1dc into 2nd ch from hook, 1htr into next ch, 1dc into next st, 1tr into next ch2, miss 4 sts, sl st into sl st at beg of round.

wing (make 2)

Using yarn B and 2.5mm (US B/1) hook, 2ch.

Round 1: (2dc, 1htr, 5dc, 1htr, 2dc) into 2nd ch from hook, sl st into 1ch at beg of round.

Break off yarn.

ASSEMBLY

Weave in loose ends, gently block and press pieces.

With wrong sides together, match up the front and back pieces and sew together around the outside.

FINISHING

Using yarn C and 2.25mm (US B/1) hook make beak as follows:

With head to the left-hand side, insert hook straight through into the 5th dc, work ch1, and then work 2dctog into the 6th and 7th dc.

Break yarn and fasten to secure.

Weave in loose ends and sew button to head for eyes, one on each side, then using picture as a guide stitch wing to body.

MATERIALS

Rowan Cotton Glace (100% cotton; approx. 115m/125yd per 50g/1¾oz ball)

A shade 849 Windsor x 1 ball

B shade 741 Poppy x 1 ball

C shade 832 Persimmon x 1 ball

Small shirt button x 1

Contrast thread for attaching eye

EQUIPMENT

Crochet hook size 2.5mm (US B/1)

GAUGE

Not crucial

FINISHED SIZE

Approx. 6cm x 4cm (2¼in x 1½in)

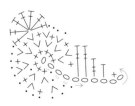

SEE DIAGRAM PAGE 120

owl

T'wit t'woo – make a little owl just for you! With its wide-set eyes and contrast bib, this design is so easy to create. The owl motif makes the perfect badge or brooch. Why not add a loop for a hanging decoration?

PATTERN

body

Using yarn A and 3mm (US D/3) hook, ch4, join ends with sl st to form ring.

Round 1: Ch1, 8dc into ring, sl st into ch1 at beg of round. (8 sts)

Round 2: Ch1, 2dc into 1st st, (1dc, 1htr) into next st, 2htr into next st, 2dc into each of the next 2 sts, 1htr into next st, (1htr, 1dc) into next st, 1dc into last st, sl st into ch1 at beg of round. (16 sts)

Round 3: Ch1, 1dc into 1st st, (2dc into next st, 1dc into next st) twice, 2htr into next st, 1htr into next st, 2dc into next st, 1dc into next st, 2dc into next st, 1htr into next st, 2htr into next st, (1dc into next st, 2dc into next st) twice, join with sl st into ch1 st beg of round. (24 sts)

Round 4: Ch1, 1dc into 1st 2 sts, work (1htr, 3dc, 1htr) into next st, sl st into each st until last st, (1htr, 3dc, 1htr) into last st, sl st into ch1 at beg of round.

Break off yarn and weave in loose ends.

SEE DIAGRAM PAGE 121

contrast centre

Using yarn B and 3mm (US D/3) hook, make magic circle, inset hook into circle and ch1.

Round 1: Work 2dc, 1htr, 2dc, 1hd, 2dc into circle, pull closed and join with sl st into ch1 at beg of round. (8 sts)

Round 2: 2dc into 1st 2 sts, (1htr, 1dc) into next st, 2dc into next st, 2dc into each of the next 2 sts, work (1dc, 1htr) into next st, 2dc into each of the last 2 sts, sl st into ch1 at beg of round. (16 sts)

Break off yarn.

beak

Using yarn C and 3mm (US D/3) hook, ch3.

Row 1: 2htr into 2nd ch from hook.

Break off yarn.

ASSEMBLY

Weave in loose ends from body and contrast centre, then block and gently press all the pieces.

Using picture as guide, place contrast centre on the right side of body and stitch into position.

Stitch eyes into position, then place beak in between eyes and sew into place using ends of yarn.

MATERIALS

Patons Cotton DK (100% cotton; approx. 210m/230yd per 100g/3½oz ball)

A shade 2738 Garnet x 1 ball

B shade 2724 Yellow x 1 ball

C shade 2723 Nectarine x 1 ball

Small shirt buttons x 2

Black thread

EQUIPMENT

Crochet hook size 3mm (US D/3)

GAUGE

Not crucial

FINISHED SIZE

Approx. 5.5cm (2in)

hedgehog

There is nothing spiky about this cute hedgehog! Made up of a main body worked in the round, then loops are added to the top section to frame the embroidered face.

PATTERN

body

Using yarn A and 3mm (US D/3) hook, ch2.

Round 1: 6dc into 2nd ch from hook, sl st into ch1 at beg of round.(6sts)

Round 2: Ch1, 1dc into each st to end, sl st into ch1 at beg of round. (6 sts)

Round 3: Ch1, 2dc into next 3 sts, 1dc into each st to end, sl st into ch1 at beg of round. (9 sts)

Round 4: Ch1, 1dc into each st to end, sl st into ch1 at beg of round.

Round 5: Ch1, 1dc into 1st st, (2dc into next st, 1dc into next st) 3 times, 1dc into each st to end, sl st into ch1 at beg of round. (12 sts)

Round 6: As round 4.

Round 7: Ch1, 1dc into 1st 2 sts, (2dc into next st, 1dc into next 2 sts) 3 times, 1dc into last st, sl st into ch1 at beg of round. (15 sts)

Round 8: Ch1, 1dc into 1st 3 sts, (2dc into next st, 1dc into next 3 sts) 3 times, sl st into ch1 at beg of round. (18 sts)

Rounds 9–14: Ch1, 1dc into back loop of each st to end, sl st into ch1 at beg of round.

Insert stuffing.

Round 15: Ch1, 1dc into 1st st, * 2dctog over next 2 sts, 1dc into next st, rep from * to last 2 sts, 2dctog over last 2 sts. (12 sts)

Round 16: Ch1, 2dctog over 1st 2 sts, * 2dctog over next 2 sts, rep from * to end. (6 sts)

Insert more stuffing if required.

Fasten off yarn leaving a tail for sewing-up.

spikes

With nose facing, join in yarn B to 1st loop next to slip stitch.

Row 1: Ch3, sl st into same st, * ch3, sl st into next st, ch3, sl st into same st, rep from * until 15 sts have been worked into, ch3, turn.

Row 2: Sl st into corresponding st on row 2, * ch3, sl st into next st, ch3, sl st into same st, rep from * until 15 sts have been worked into, ch3, turn.

Repeat round 2 until you reach round 15 of body (1st decrease round), then work a further 2 rows of spikes keeping the spike pattern correct.

FINISHING

Using picture as a guide, embroider facial features onto hedgehog as follows: First, work the triangular nose shape to the very front using pink embroidery thread and satin stitch, then attach the eyes using black embroidery thread and French knot stitch, wrapping the thread round needle approx. 4 times.

MATERIALS

Rowan Felted Tweed DK (50% merino wool, 25% alpaca, 25% viscose; approx. 175m/191yd per 50g/1¾oz ball)

A shade 160 Gilt x 1 ball

Rowan Fine Tweed (100% wool; approx. 90m/98yd per 25g/1oz ball)

B shade 373 Dent x 1 ball

Polyester toy stuffing

Black and pink embroidery thread for facial features

EQUIPMENT

Crochet hook size 3mm (US D/3)

Embroidery needle

GAUGE

Not crucial

FINISHED SIZE

Approx. 5.5cm (2in) long, 12cm (4¾in) circumference

mouse pincushion

Pincushions are an essential part of a crafter's kit, so what's better than making your own? Worked in the round and stuffed with polyester toy stuffing, the ears are crocheted separately then stitched into position.

PATTERN

body

Using 4mm (US G/6) hook, ch2.

Round 1: 6dc into 2nd ch from hook, sl st into ch1 at beg of round. (6 sts)

Round 2: Ch1, 1dc into each st to end, sl st into ch1 at beg of round.

Round 3: Ch1, 2dc into next 3 sts, 1dc into each st to end, sl st into ch1 at beg of round. (9 sts)

Round 4: Ch1, 1dc into each st to end, sl st into ch1 at beg of round.

Round 5: Ch1, 1dc into 1st st, (2dc into next st, 1dc into next st) 3 times, 1dc into each st to end, sl st into ch1 at beg of round. (12 sts)

Round 6: As round 4.

Round 7: Ch1, 1dc into 1st 2 sts, (2dc into next st, 1dc into next 2 sts) 3 times, 1dc into last st, sl st into ch1 at beg of round. (15 sts)

Round 8: Ch1, 1dc into 1st 3 sts, (2dc into next st, 1dc into next 3 sts) 3 times, sl st into ch1 at beg of round. (18 sts)

Round 9: Ch1, 1dc into 1st 4 sts, (2dc into next st, 1dc into next 4 sts) twice, 2dc into next st, 1dc into each st to end, sl st into ch1 at beg of round. (21 sts)

Round 10: Ch1, 1dc into 1st 5 sts, work (2dc into next st, 1dc into next 5 sts) twice, 2dc into next st,

1dc into each st to end, sl st into ch1 at beg of round. (24 sts)

Rounds 11–17: As round 4.

Insert stuffing.

Round 18: Ch1, 1dc into 1st 2 sts, * 2dctog over next 2 sts, 1dc into next 2 sts, rep from * to last 2 sts, 2dctog over last 2 sts, sl st into ch1 at beg of round. (18 sts)

Round 19: Ch1, 1dc into 1st st, * 2dctog over next 2 sts, 1dc into next st, rep from * to last 2 sts, 2dctog over last 2 sts, sl st into ch1 at beg of round. (12 sts)

Round 20: Ch1, 2dctog over 1st 2 sts, * 2dctog over next 2 sts, rep from * to end. (6 sts)

Insert more stuffing if required.

Sew opening closed and weave in ends.

tail

Ch25, turn and sl st into each ch to end.

Fasten off yarn leaving long enough length to sew up opening.

ears (make 2)

Using 4 mm (US G/6) hook, ch4.

Row 1: 5dc into 4th ch from hook, ch3, sl st into same ch dc's worked into.

Fasten off yarn leaving a long enough tail to stitch ears to body.

MATERIALS

Brown Sheep Lamb's Pride Worsted (85% wool, 15% mohair; approx. 173m/190yd per 100g/3½oz ball) shade 0123 Limeade x 1 ball

EQUIPMENT

Crochet hook size 4mm (US G/6)

Black and pink embroidery thread for facial features

Polyester toy stuffing

GAUGE

Approx 18 sts x 20 rows = 10cm (4in) in double crochet

FINISHED SIZE

Approx. 11cm (4¼in) long, 12.5cm (5in) circumference

ASSEMBLY

Using picture as a guide, sew ears and tail into position on body.

Embroider facial features as follows:

Work the triangular nose shape to the very front using pink embroidery thread and satin stitch. Next attach the eyes using black embroidery thread and French knot stitch, wrapping the thread around needle approx. 4 times.

Weave in all loose ends.

owl mask

This is a neat costume mask. The wide eyes are worked in the round from a figure 8, with the contrast outer built up using increasing and decreasing techniques that also help shape the nose. Everything is held snug and secure with a flat elastic strap to the back.

PATTERN

Using yarn A and 3.5mm (US E/4) hook, create figure 8 base for mask as follows:

Round 1: Ch22, sl st into 1st chain to form loop, ch28, miss 21ch, sl st into next ch to form loop, then work 1dc into next 7ch in between the 2 loops.

Round 2: Sl st into 1st 20ch loop, ch1, then work 48dc into loop, work 1dc into underside of ch7, work 48dc into 2nd 20ch loop, 1dc into next 7 sts, sl st into ch1 at beg of round. (110 sts)

Break off yarn and join in yarn B.

Round 3: Ch1, 1dc into next 4 sts, 2dc into next st, 1htr into next 4 sts, 2htr into next st, (1dc into next 4 sts, 2dc into next st) twice, 1htr into next 4 sts, 2htr into next st, (1dc into next 4 sts, 2dc into next st) twice, place marker at 1st increase, 1dc into next 15 sts, (2dc into next st, 1dc into next 4 sts) twice, place marker at 2nd increase, 2htr into stitch, 1htr into next 4 sts, (2dc into next st, 1dc into next 4 sts) twice, 2htr into next st, 1htr into next 4 sts, 2dc into next st, 1dc into next 6 sts, work 3dctog over next 3 sts, 1dc into last 2 sts, sl st into ch 1 at beg of row. (104 sts)

Round 4: Ch1, 1dc into next 6 sts, 1htr into next 6 sts, 1dc into next 12 sts, 1htr into next 6 sts, 1dc into next 14 sts, 2dctog over next 2 sts, 1dc into next 5 sts, 2dctog over next 2 sts, 1dc into next 14 sts, 1htr into next 6 sts, 1dc into next 12 sts, 1htr into next 6 sts, 1dc into next 7 sts, 3dctog over next 3 sts, 1dc into last st, sl st into ch1 at beg of round. (98 sts)

Break off yarn B.

With right side facing, join in yarn C at stitch that matches up with marker.

Next row: Ch1, 1dc into next 5 sts, 1htr into next 6 sts, 1dc into next 12 sts, 1htr into next 6 sts, 1dc into next 4 sts, 2htr into next 2 sts, 3dctog over next 3 sts, 2htr into next 2 sts, 1dc into next 4 sts, 1htr into next 6 sts, 1dc into next 12 sts, 1htr into next 6 sts, 1dc into next 5 sts, turn. (75 sts)

Next row: Sl st into 1st 3 sts, 1dc into next 3 sts, 1htr into next 6 sts, 2dc into next st, 1dc into next 5 sts, 1htr into next 6 sts, 1dc into next 8 sts, 3dctog over next 3 sts, 1dc into next 8 sts, 1htr into next 6 sts, 1dc into next 5 sts, 2dc into next st, 1htr into next 6 sts, 1dc into next 3 sts, sl st into last 3 sts. (61 sts)
Break off yarn.

ears (make 2)

Using yarn C and 3.5mm (US E/4) hook, ch4 and join together with sl st to form a ring.

Row 1: Ch1, 5dc into ring, turn. (5 sts)

Row 2: Ch1, 2dc into each of the 1st 2 sts, 3dc into next st, 2dc into each st to end, turn. (11 sts)

Row 3: Ch1, 1dc into 1st st, (2dc into next st, 1dc into next st) twice, 3dc into next st, work (1dc into next st, 2dc into next st) twice, 1dc into last st, turn. (17 sts)

beak

Using yarn D and 3.5mm (US E/4) hook, ch10 + 1 turning ch.

Row 1: 1dc into 2nd ch from hook, 2dctog over next ch2, 1dc into next ch4, 2dctog over next 2 sts, 1dc into last st, turn.

Row 2: Ch1, 1dc into 1st st, 2dctog over next 2 sts, 1dc into next 2 sts, 1dctog over next 2 sts, 1dc into last st, turn.

Row 3: Ch1, 1dc into 1st st, (2dctog over next 2 sts) twice, 1dc into last st, turn.

Row 4: Ch1, 1dc into 1st st, 2dctog over next 2 sts, 1dc into next st, turn.

Row 5: Ch2, (1htr, 1dc, 1htr) together over last 3 sts.

Break off yarn.

ASSEMBLY

Weave in loose ends, then block and press main owl mask, ears and beak – note that the mask fabric will need to be pinned out around the top outer edge, leaving a bump free for the shaping at the lower nose.

Using picture as guide, stitch ears and beak into position.

Cut elastic to the correct length for a snug fit and sew into position on the inside of the mask.

animal ears

This will be a fancy dress-up favourite with kids and adults alike. The ears are quick and simple to make and a great way to get familiar with different basic stitches for creating shapes. Why not change the colour and shape for different animals?

PATTERN

outer ear (make 2)

Using yarn A and 4mm (US G/6) hook, ch4 and join together with sl st to form a ring.

Row 1: Ch1, 5dc into ring, turn. (5 sts)

Row 2: Ch1, 2dc into each of the 1st 2 sts, 3dc into next st, 2dc into each st to end, turn. (11 sts)

Row 3: Ch1, 1dc into 1st st, (2dc into next st, 1dc into next st) twice, 3dc into next st, (1dc into next st, 2dc into next st) twice, 1dc into last st, turn. (17 sts)

Row4 : Ch1, 1dc into 1st 3 sts, 2htr into next st, 1htr into next 4 sts, 3dc into next st, 1htr into next 4 sts, 2htr into next st, 1dc into last 3 sts, turn. (21 sts)

Row 5: Ch1, 1dc into 1st 4 sts, 2htr into next st, 1htr into next 5 sts, 3dc into next st, 1htr into next 5 sts, 2htr into next st, 1dc into last 4 sts, turn. (25 sts)

inner ear (make 2)

Using yarn B and 4mm (US G/6) hook, ch4 and join together with sl st to form a ring.

Row 1: Ch1, 5dc into ring, turn. (5 sts)

Row 2: Ch1, 2dc into 1st st, 2htr nto next st, 3dc into next st, 2htr into next st, 2dc into last st, turn. (11 sts)

Row 3: Ch1, 1dc into 1st st, 2dc into next st, 1htr into next st, 2htr into next st, 1dc into next st, 3dc into next st, 1dc into next st, 2htr into next st, 1htr into next st, 2dc into next st, 1dc into last st, turn. (17 sts)

Fasten off yarn.

ASSEMBLY

Weave in loose ends, then gently block and press.

Sew pink inner ear to the outer ear, matching up the centre rings.

FINISHING

Using yarn B and 3mm (US D/3) hook, make tie as follows:

Ch100, work 13dc across bottom of 1st ear, ch8, work 13dc across bottom of 2nd ear, ch100.

Fasten off yarn.

Weave in loose ends.

MATERIALS

Rowan Creative Focus Worsted (75% wool, 25% alpaca; approx. 200m/220yd per 100g/3½oz ball)

A shade 0500 Ebony x 1

B shade 2055 Carmine x 1

EQUIPMENT

Crochet hook size 4mm (US G/6)

Crochet hook size 3mm (US D/3)

GAUGE

Approx. 18 sts x 20 rows = 10cm (4in) in double crochet

FINISHED SIZE

Each ear approx. 7cm (2¾in) wide, 5.5cm (2in) deep

snowflake

This magical snowflake shape is not just for Christmas. Worked in the round using a variety of stitches to create the shape, it's a good project for practising your skills.

PATTERN

Using 2mm (US B/1) hook and yarn A, ch7, join ends together with sl st to form loop.

Round 1: Ch1, 16dc into ring, join with sl st into ch1 at beg of round.

Round 2: Sl st into top of 1st st, * ch4, sl st into next st, rep from * 14 more times, ch1 sl st into base of 1st ch4 loop. (16 loops)

Round 3: Sl st into 1st ch2 of ch4 loop, ch1, * 1dc into same loop, ch6, miss next ch4 loop, work 1dc into next ch4 loop, rep from * ending last rep with sl st into ch1 at beg of round. (8 loops)

Round 4: Sl st into 1st ch3 of ch6 loop, ch1, * 1dc into same loop, ch8, 1dc into next ch6 loop, rep from * ending last rep with sl st into ch1 at beg of round. (8 loops)

Round 5: ch1,* work (3dc, 2htr, 1dc) into ch8 loop, make large spike picot as follows, (ch6, 1dc into 4th ch from hook) 3 times, (ch4, 1sl st into base of last dc) twice, (sl st into next ch2 and base of next dc, ch4 sl st into base of same dc) twice, sl st into last 2ch (large spike picot worked), (1dc, 2htr, 3dc) into same ch8 loop, 6dc into next ch8 loop, make small picot spike as follows, (ch6, 1dc into 4th ch from hook) twice, (ch4, 1sl st into base of last dc) twice, sl st into next ch2 and base of next dc, ch4 sl st into base of same dc, sl st into last 2ch (small spike picot worked), 6dc into same ch8 loop, rep from * 3 more times, sl st into ch1 at beg of round. The large and small spikes should alternate around the motif.

Fasten off yarn.

FINISHING

Weave in loose ends, then block and press to flatten crochet and stretch out picots. Add a ribbon or thread for hanging.

SEE DIAGRAM PAGE 121

MATERIALS

Coats Anchor Artiste 10 count (100% mercerized cotton; approx. 274m/ 299yd per 50g/ 1¾oz ball), shade 1 White x 1 ball

EQUIPMENT

Crochet hook size 2mm (US B/1)

GAUGE

Not crucial

FINISHED SIZE

Approx. 10cm (4in) wide

cup cosy

Show your true stripes with this chevron cup cosy. Slip onto your carry-out cup to protect your fingers and keep in the heat. It's a good project for practising increasing and decreasing while creating a funky zig-zag fabric.

MATERIALS

Rowan Cotton Glacé (100% cotton; approx. 115m/125yd per 50g/1¾oz ball)

A shade 856 Mineral x 1 ball

B shade 814 Shoot x 1 ball

C shade 858 Aqua x 1 ball

Rowan Siena 4 ply (100% cotton; approx. 140m/ 153yd per 50g/1¾oz ball)

D shade 680 Lipstick x 1 ball

E shade 658 Floret x 1 ball

EQUIPMENT

Crochet hook size 3mm (US B/2)

GAUGE

Approx. 32 sts x 32 rows = 10cm (4in) in double crochet

FINISHED SIZE

Width at bottom approx. 18cm (7in), top 24cm (9½in), length 8cm (3in)

◄ projects

PATTERN

Using yarn A and 3mm (US B/2) hook, ch59.

Row 1: Ch1, 1dc into each ch to end, turn.

Row 2: Ch1, 1dc into 1st st, 2dctog over next 2 sts, *1dc into next 4 sts, 2dc into next st, 1dc into next st, 2dc into next st, 1sc into next 4 sts**, 3dctog over next 3 sts; rep from * ending last rep at **, 2dctog over next 2 sts, 1dc into last st, turn.

Fasten off yarn A and join in yarn B.

Rows 3–4: As row 2.

Break off yarn B and join in yarn C.

Row 5: As row 2.

Row 6: Ch1, 1dc into 1st 6 sts, *2dc into next st, 1dc into next st, 2dc into next st **, 1dc into next 9 sts, rep from * ending last rep at **, 1dc into each st to end, turn. (67 sts)

Break off yarn C and join in yarn D.

Row 7: Ch1, 1dc into 1st st, 2dctog over next 2 sts, *1dc into next 5 sts, 2dc into next st, 1dc into next st, 2dc into next st, 1sc into next 5 sts**, 3dctog over next 3 sts, rep from * ending last rep at ** 2dctog over next 2 sts, 1dc into last st, turn.

Row 8: as row 7.

Break off yarn D and join in yarn E.

Rows 9–10: As row 7.

FINISHING

Weave in loose ends, block and press, making sure you pin out all the peaks at the top and bottom.

Sew the short straight ends together and secure the top and bottom with a few stitches.

container with handle

Keep the clutter at bay with this little container. Worked in the round to make a square shape, with deep sides and a handle worked in double crochet. The base has a slight lip to help it sit nice and flat.

INTERMEDIATE

PATTERN

pot

Using 2 ends together throughout and 6mm (US J/10) hook, use magic circle technique.

Round 1: Ch1, 12dc into magic loop, sl st into ch1 at beg of round. (12 sts)

Round 2: Ch1, 1dc into 1st 2 sts, * 3dc into next st, 1dc into next 2 sts, rep from * twice more, 3dc into last st, sl st into ch1 at beg of round. (20 sts)

Round 3: Ch1, 1dc into 1st 3 sts, * 3dc into next st, 1dc into next 4 sts, rep from * twice more, 3dc into next st, 1dc into last st, sl st into ch1 at beg of round. (28 sts)

Round 4: Ch1, 1sc into 1st 4 sts, * 3dc into next st, 1dc into next 6 sts, rep from * twice more, 3dc into next st, 1dc into last 2 sts, sl st into ch1 at beg of round. (36 sts)

Round 5: Ch1, 1dc into 1st 5 sts, * 3dc into next st, 1dc into next 8 sts, rep from * twice more, 3dc into next st, 1dc into last 3 sts, sl st into ch1 at beg of round. (42 sts)

Round 6: Ch1, work 1dc around the stem of each stitch instead of into top of stitch to end, sl st into ch1 at beg of round.

Round 7: Ch1, 1dc into each st to end, sl st into ch1 at beg of round.

Repeat round 7 a further 10 times. Break off yarn.

handle

Using 6mm (US J/10) hook, ch5.

Row 1: 1dc into 2nd ch from hook, 1dc into each ch to end, turn. (4 sts)

Row 2: Ch1, 1dc into each st to end, turn.

Repeat last row a further 18 times. Break off yarn.

ASSEMBLY

Fold corners of pot, then press with steam iron and damp cloth to help define square shape.

Sew handle to top of pot making sure it sits at the centre of the opposite sides.

Weave in loose ends.

MATERIALS

Rowan Denim (100% cotton; approx. 100m/ 109yd per 50g/1¾oz ball), shade 324 Ecru x 1 ball

EQUIPMENT

Crochet hook size 6mm (US size J/10)

GAUGE

Approx. 12 sts x 14 rows = 10cm (4in) in double crochet

FINISHED SIZE

Approx. 10cm x 9cm (4in x 3½in)

glass stem marker

Using a glass stem marker is a pretty way to keep an eye on which glass is yours at a party. The design is made by covering craft wire with double crochet and beads, and the mixture of seed and teardrop beads sits perfectly around the stem and onto the base of the glass.

PATTERN

Using your chosen colour of yarn thread beads onto yarn as follows:

Thread sewing needle with approx. 15cm (6in) of sewing thread and knot the ends together to form a loop. Insert end of yarn into loop, then thread beads, in the following sequence, onto the needle, down the thread and onto the yarn: 2 seed beads, 1 teardrop, (3 seed beads, 1 teardrop) twice, 2 seed beads. Remember, the 1st bead you thread on will be the last bead you work.

Cut length of wire approx 11cm (4½in) long and using the bottle nose pliers, bend over the ends to form loops.

Using 2mm (US B/1) hook join yarn to wire as follows:

Make slip knot and place on hook, insert hook under wire, yarn round hook and draw loop through (2 loops on hook), yarn round hook and draw through loops, ch1, work 31sc, turn.

Next row: Ch1, 1sl st into 1st 6 sts, work next 19 sts with beads as follows, insert hook into next st, yarn round hook and draw loop through, bring bead up to back of work and finish stitch off as normal, once all 19 sts have been worked, sl st into last 6 sts.

Break off yarn.

FINISHING

Weave in loose ends and bring the loops at either end of the wire and link together.

MATERIALS

Anchor Pearl Cotton No 8 (100% cotton; approx. 85m/ 93yd per 10g/⅓oz ball)

A shade Bright blue x 1 ball

B shade Red x 1 ball

Medium florist wire, approx. 30cm (12in)

Seed beads x 10

Teardrop beads x 3

EQUIPMENT

Crochet hook size 2mm (US B/1)

Pair of bottle nose pliers

Sharp sewing needle & sewing thread

GAUGE

Not crucial

FINISHED SIZE

2.5cm (1in)

snug coaster

Colour code your drinks with these snug coasters, designed to fit around the average stemmed glass. The shape is worked in one piece, in the round, using increase and decrease stitches.

MATERIALS

Rowan Cotton Glacé (100% cotton; approx. 115m/125yd per 50g/1¾oz ball), shade 851 Ultramarine x 1 ball

EQUIPMENT

Crochet hook size 3mm (US D/3)

GAUGE

Approx. 20 sts x 20 rows = 10cm (4in) in double crochet

FINISHED SIZE

Approx. 8cm (3in)

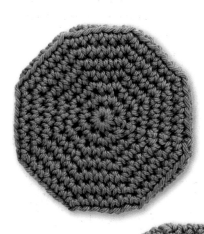

PATTERN

Using 3mm (US D/3) hook, ch4, join ends together to form ring.

Round 1: Ch1, 8dc into ring, sl st into ch1 at beg of round. (8 sts)

Round 2: Ch1, 2dc into each st. (16 sts)

Round 3: Ch1, 1dc into 1st st, * 2dc into next st, 1dc into next st, rep from * to last st, 2dc into last st, sl st into ch1 at beg of round. (24 sts)

Round 4: Ch1, 1dc into 1st 2 sts, * 2dc into next st, 1dc into next 2 sts, rep from * to last st, 2dc into last st, sl st into ch1 at beg of round. (32 sts)

Round 5: Ch1, 1dc into 1st 3 sts, * 2dc into next st, 1dc into next 3 sts, rep from * to last st, 2dc into last st, sl st into ch1 at beg of round. (40 sts)

Round 6: Ch1, 1dc into 1st 4 sts, * 2dc into next st, 1dc into next 4 sts, rep from * to last st, 2dc into last st, sl st into ch1 at beg of round. (48 sts)

Round 7: Ch1, 1dc into 1st 5 sts, * 2dc into next st, 1dc into next 5 sts, rep from * to last st, 2dc into last st, sl st into ch1 at beg of round. (56 sts)

Round 8: Working into back loop of sts, ch1, 1dc into 1st 5 sts, * 2dctog over next 2 sts, 1dc into next 5 sts, rep from * to last 2 sts, 2dctog over last 2 sts, sl st into ch1 at beg of round. (48 sts)

Round 9: Ch1, 1dc into 1st 4 sts, * 2dctog over next 2 sts, 1dc into next 4 sts, rep from * to last 2 sts, 2dctog over last 2 sts, sl st into ch1 at beg of round. (40 sts)

Round 10: Ch1, 1dc into 1st 3 sts, * 2dctog over next 2 sts, 1dc into next 3 sts, rep from * to last 2 sts, 2dctog over last 2 sts, sl st into ch1 at beg of round. (32 sts)

Round 11: Ch1, 1dc into 1st 2 sts, * 2dctog over next 2 sts, 1dc into next 2 sts, rep from * to last 2 sts, 2dctog over last 2 sts, sl st into ch1 at beg of round. (24 sts)

Fasten off yarn.

FINISHING

Weave in loose ends and gently block and press to measurements.

plant pot

This container is perfect for hanging on pegs or door handles. Crocheted in natural sheep breeds wool, it will withstand the outdoors and all the weather can throw at it, so why not pot up your plants and watch them grow.

MATERIALS

Brown Sheep Lamb's Pride Bulky (85% wool, 15% mohair, approx. 110m/120yd per 100g/3½oz ball), shade 0107 Lemon Drop x 1 ball

EQUIPMENT

Crochet hook size 6.5mm (US K/10)

GAUGE

Approx. 12 sts x 14 rows = 10cm (4in) in double crochet

FINISHED SIZE

Approx. 11cm x 12.5cm (4¼in x 5in), circumference 37cm (14½in)

PATTERN

Using 6.5mm (US H/8) hook, ch4, join ends together with sl st.

Round 1: Ch1, 8dc into ring, sl st into ch1 at beg of round. (8 sts)

Round 2: 2dc into each st, sl st into ch1 at beg of round. (16 sts)

Round 3: Ch1, 1dc into 1st st, * 2dc into next st, 1dc into next st, rep from * to last st, 2dc into last st, sl st into ch1 at beg of round. (24 sts)

Round 4: Ch1, 1dc into 1st 2 sts, * 2dc into next st, 1dc into next 2 sts, rep from * to last st, 2dc into last st, sl st into ch1 at beg of round. (32 sts)

Round 5: Ch1, 1dc into 1st 3 sts, * 2dc into next st, 1dc into next 3 sts, rep from * to last st, 2dc into last st, sl st into ch1 at beg of round. (40 sts)

Round 6: Ch1, work 1dc around stem of each st to end, sl st into ch1 at beg of round.

Round 7: Ch1, 1dc into each st to end, sl st into ch1 at beg of round.

Repeat round 7 a further 13 times.

Work handle as follows:

Next round: Ch1, 1dc into next 15 sts, ch10, miss 10, 1dc into each st to end, sl st into ch1 at beg of round.

Next round: Ch1, 1dc into next 15 sts, 1dc into each of the next ch10, 1dc into each st to end

Next round: As round 7.

Fasten off yarn.

FINISHING

Weave in ends.

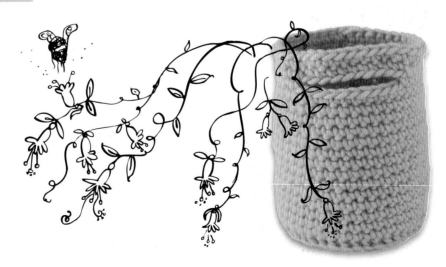

string bag bottle holder

Keep your water bottle handy at all times with this string bag-inspired bottle holder, worked in the round using a combination of chains, double crochet and slip stitches to make a net fabric. The top is closed with a simple drawstring.

PATTERN

bag

Using 3.5mm (US E/4) hook, ch5 and join ends with sl st to form ring.

Round 1: Ch1, * 1dc into ring, ch5, rep from * 10 more times, sl st into ch1 at beg of round. (11 loops)

Round 2: Sl st into 1st 3 ch of first loop, ch1, 1dc into same loop, * ch7, 1dc into next loop, rep from * ending last rep with sl st into ch1 at beg of round.

Rep round 2 a further 9 times.

Round 12: Sl st into 1st 3 ch of first loop, ch1, 1dc into same loop, * ch5, 1dc into next loop, rep from * ending last rep with sl st into ch1 at beg of round.

Round 13: Sl st into 1st 3 ch of first loop, ch1, 1dc into same loop, * ch3, 1dc into next loop, rep from * ending last rep with sl st into ch1 at beg of round.

Fasten off yarn.

drawstring

Using 3.5mm (US E/4) hook and cotton yarn, work a chain to the required length.

Weave chain in and out of the top ch3 loops then either sew or knot ends together.

FINISHING

Weave in loose ends.

MATERIALS

Patons Cotton DK (100% cotton; approx. 210m/230yd per 100g/ 3½oz ball), shade 2697 Denim x 1 ball

EQUIPMENT

Crochet hook size 3.5mm (US E/4)

GAUGE

Not crucial

FINISHED SIZE

Approx. 18cm x 9cm (7in x 3½in)

napkin rings

Add a personal touch to your dining table with these lace trim napkin rings, perfect for adding a splash of colour to the table. The design is worked around a plastic ring then layers of lace are built up on one side in contrasting colours.

MATERIALS

Rowan Cotton Glacé (100% cotton; approx. 115m/ 125yd per 50g/1¾oz ball)

A shade 741 Poppy/837 Baked Red/445 Blood Orange x 1 ball

B shade 724 Bubbles/856 Mineral/841 Garnet x 1 ball

4cm (1½in) plastic ring for each napkin ring

EQUIPMENT

Crochet hook size 3mm (US D/3)

GAUGE

Not crucial

FINISHED SIZE

Approx. 9cm x 7cm (3½in x 2¾in)

PATTERN

Using yarn A and 3mm (US D/3) hook, cover plastic ring as follows:

Make slip knot and place on hook, insert hook through centre of hook, yarn around hook and draw loop through (2 loops on hook), yarn around hook and draw through both loops, ch1, work 44dc crochet around ring, sl st into ch1 at beg of round.

Work trim as follows: ch2 (counts as 1dc), 1tr into 1st st, ch2, 2trtog into same st, *ch1, misr 2 sts, work (2trtog, ch2, 2trtog) into next st, rep from * 3 more times.

Break off yarn A and join in yarn B.

Next row: Ch1, 1sc into top of 1st 2trtog, * work (1dc, 1htr, 1tr, 1dtr, 1tr, 1htr, 1dc) into ch2sp, 1dc in between next 2trtog, rep from * to end, working last dc into top of last 2trtog.

FINISHING

Weave in loose ends, then pin out fancy trim and ring, spray with water and leave to dry.

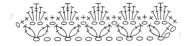

SEE DIAGRAM PAGE 121

fancy jam jar cover

Turn a simple jam jar into a pretty vase. The lace effect fabric is worked in the round and stretched slightly around the jar to get the full effect. Add a tea light to cast a lacy shadow.

PATTERN

Using 4mm (US G/6) hook, ch5, join ends together with sl st to form a ring.

Round 1: Ch6 (counts as 1dc and ch3), * 1tr into ring, ch3, rep from * 4 more times, sl st into 3rd ch at beg of round.

Round 2: Sl st into 1st ch3 sp, ch3 (counts as 1tr), 3tr into same ch3sp, * ch3, 4tr into next ch3sp, rep from * to end, sl st into top of ch3 at beg of round.

Round 3: Sl st across 3dc and into next ch3sp, ch3 (counts as 1tr), work (1tr, ch3, 2tr) into same ch3 sp, ch3, * work (2tr, ch3, 2tr) into next ch3sp, ch3, rep from * to end, sl st into top of ch3 at beg of round.

Round 4: Sl st into 1st dc and into ch3sp, ch3 (counts as 1tr), work (1tr, ch3, 2tr) into same ch3sp, * ch1, 1tr into next ch3sp, ch1 **, work (2tr, ch3, 2tr) into next ch3sp, rep from * ending last rep at **, sl st into top of ch3 at beg of round.

Round 5: Sl st into 1st tr and into ch3sp, ch3 (counts as 1tr), work (1tr, ch3, 2tr) into same ch3 sp, * ch1, work 2trtog inserting hook into each of the next ch1 sp, ch1**, work (2tr, ch3, 2tr) into next ch3sp, rep from * ending last rep at **, sl st into top of ch3 at beg of round.

Round 6: Sl st into 1st tr and into ch3sp, ch3 (counts as 1tr), work (1tr, ch3, 2tr) into same ch3sp, * ch1, miss ch1, 1tr into top of 2trtog, miss ch1, ch1 **, work (2tr, ch3, 2tr) into next ch3sp, rep from * ending last rep at **, sl st into top of ch3 at beg of round.

Repeat rounds 5 and 6 twice more then round 5 once more.

Next round: Ch1, work 1dc into top of ch3 of prev round and next st, 3dc into next ch3 sp, * 1dc into next 2 sts, 1dc into next ch1sp, miss next st, 1dc into next ch1sp **, 1dc into next 2 sts, 3dc into ch3sp, 1dc into next 2 sts, rep from * ending last rep at **, sl st into ch1 at beg of round.

drawstring

Using 4mm (US G/6) hook, ch250, loop through the 1st and 4th gaps at the top edge. Sew or knot ends together.

FINISHING

Weave in loose ends.

If using with a candle, please use suitable wire for hanging – check that the wire will withstand the heat.

MATERIALS
Rowan Siena 4 ply (100% cotton, approx. 140m/153yd per 50g/1¾oz ball), shade 652 Cream x 1 ball

EQUIPMENT
Crochet hook size 4mm (US G/6)

GAUGE
Approx. 2 pattern repeats = 8cm (3in) and 8 rows = 10cm (4in)

FINISHED SIZE
Approx. 6.5cm x 9cm (2½in x 3½in)

place mat

Bring your crochet skills to the table with this fun place mat which allows you to play around with colours and make some stripes. Worked in 100% cotton, they can easily be popped in the washer as necessary.

PATTERN

Using 2 ends together throughout
ch22 + 1 turning chain.

Row 1: 1dc into 2nd ch from hook, 1dc into each ch to end, turn. (22 sts)

Row 2: Ch1, 1dc into each st to end.

Work all following rows as row 2 in the following stripe sequence:

Rows 3–5: Yarn A.
Rows 6–9: Yarn B.
Rows 10–12: Yarn C.
Rows 13–14: Yarn D.
Row 15: Yarn E.
Rows 16–17: Yarn D.
Rows 18–20: Yarn C.
Rows 21–24: Yarn B.
Rows 25–29: Yarn A.

FINISHING

Weave in loose ends, then block and press to correct size.

MATERIALS

Brown Sheep Nature Spun Worsted (100% wool; approx. 224m/245yd per 100g/3½oz ball)

A shade 040 Turquoise Wonder x 1 ball

B shade 003 Lemon Grasl st x 1 ball

C shade 052 French Clay x 1 ball

D shade 054 Impasl ste Yellow x 1 ball

E shade 0188 Snow x 1 ball

EQUIPMENT

Crochet hook size 5mm (US H/8)

GAUGE

Approx. 14 sts x 15 rows = 10cm (4in) in double crochet with yarn held double

FINISHED SIZE

Approx. 15cm x 20cm (6in x 8in)

circle to square coaster

The coaster is worked in the round, changing colour so you can see the circle turn into a square.

PATTERN

Using 3.5mm (US E/4) hook and yarn A, make magic circle.

Round 1: Ch1, work 8dc into loop, join with sl st into ch1 at beg of round. (8 sts)

Round 2: Ch1, 2htr into 1st st, 2htr into each st to end, join with sl st into ch1 at beg of round. (16 sts)

Fasten off yarn A and join in yarn B.

Round 3: Ch2, 1htr into 1st st, * 2htr into next st, 1htr into next st, rep from * to last st, 2htr into last st, join with sl st into last st. (24 sts)

Round 4: Ch2, 1htr into 1st 2 sts, * 2htr into next st, 1htr into next 2 sts, rep from * to last st, 2htr into last st, join with sl st into last st. (32 sts)

Fasten off yarn B and join in yarn C.

Round 5: Ch2, 1htr into 1st 3 sts, * 2htr into next st, 1htr into next 3 sts, rep from * to last st, 2htr into last st, join with sl st into last st. (40 sts)

Round 6: Ch1, 1dc into 1st st, 1htr into next 2 sts, 1tr into next st, 3tr into next st (corner worked), * 1tr into next st, 1htr into next 2 sts, 1dc into next 3 sts, 1htr into next 2 sts, 1tr into next st, 3tr into next st (corner worked), rep from * twice more, 1tr into next st, 1htr into next st, 1dc into next 2 sts, join with sl st into ch1 at beg of round. (48 sts)

Fasten off yarn C and join in yarn D.

Round 7: Ch1, 1dc into 1st 2 sts, 1htr into next 2 sts, 1tr into next st, 3tr into next st (corner worked), * 1tr into next st, 1htr into next 2 sts, 1dc into next 5 sts, 1htr into next 2 sts, 1tr into next st, 3tr into next st (corner worked), rep from * twice more, 1tr into next st, 1htr into next st, 1dc into next 3 sts, join with sl st into ch1 at beg of round. (56 sts)

Fasten off yarn D and join in yarn E.

Round 8: Ch1, 1dc into 1st 5 sts, 1htr into next st, 3tr into next st (corner worked), * 1htr into next st, 1dc into next 11 sts, 1htr into next st, 3tr into next st (corner worked), rep from * twice more, 1htr into next st, 1dc into last 6 sts, join with sl st into ch1 at beg of round.

FINISHING

Weave in loose ends, block and press to measurements.

MATERIALS

Patons Cotton DK (100% cotton; approx. 210m/ 230yd per 100g/3½oz ball)

A shade 2743 Purple x 1 ball

B shade 2733 Grape x 1 ball

C shade 2724 Pomegranate x 1 ball

D shade 2725 Pink x 1 ball

E shade 2724 Yellow x 1 ball

EQUIPMENT

Crochet hook size 3.5 mm (US E/4)

GAUGE

Approx. 15 sts x 15 rows = 10cm (4in) in double crochet

FINISHED SIZE

Approx. 9cm x 9cm (3½in x 3½in)

granny square table runner

The granny square is such a versatile shape and can be used in so many ways. This design uses a larger motif stitched together to make a table runner.

PATTERN (MAKE 9)

Using yarn A and 4mm (US G/6) hook, ch 4, join ends together with sl st to form ring.

Round 1: Ch6 (counts as 1dc and ch3), * 3tr into ring, ch3 rep from * twice more, 2tr into ring, join with sl st into 3rd of ch6 at beg of round. Sl st into 1st ch3sp. (4 sets of 3dc)

Fasten off yarn A and join in yarn B.

Round 2: Ch6 (counts as 1tr and ch3), work 3tr into 1st ch3sp, * ch1, work (3tr, 3ch, 3tr) into next ch3sp, rep from * twice more, 2tr into 1st ch3sp, sl st 3rd of ch6 at beg of round. Sl st into ch3sp. (8 sets of 3dc)

Fasten off yarn B and join in yarn C.

Round 3: Ch6 (counts as 1tr and ch3), work 3tr into 1st ch3sp, * ch1, 3tr into next ch1sp, work (3tr, 3ch, 3tr) into next ch3sp, rep from * twice more, ch1, 3tr into next ch1sp, 2tr into 1st ch3sp, sl st into 3rd of ch6 at beg of round. Sl st into ch3sp. (12 sets of 3tr)

Fasten off yarn C and join in yarn D.

Round 4: Ch6 (counts as 1tr and ch3), work 3tr into 1st ch3sp, * work (ch1, 3tr into next ch1sp) twice, ch1, work (3tr, 3ch, 3tr) into next ch3sp, rep from * twice more, work (ch1, 3tr into next ch1sp) twice, ch1, 2tr into ch3sp, sl st into 3rd of ch6 at beg of round. Sl st into ch3sp. (16 sets of 3dc)

Fasten off yarn D and join in yarn E.

Round 5: Ch6 (counts as 1tr and ch3), work 3tr into 1st ch3sp, * work (ch1, 3tr into next ch1sp) 3 times, ch1, work (3tr, 3ch, 3tr) into next ch3sp, rep from * twice more, work (ch1, 3tr into next ch1sp) 3 times, ch1, 2tr into ch3sp, sl st into 3rd of ch6 at beg of round. Sl st into ch3sp. (20 sets of 3tr)

Round 6: Ch6 (counts as 1tr and ch3), work 3tr into 1st ch3sp, * work (ch1, 3tr into next ch1sp) 4 times, ch1, work (3tr, 3ch, 3tr) into next ch3sp, rep from * twice more, work (ch1, 3tr into next ch1sp) 4 times, ch1, 2tr into ch3sp, sl st into 3rd of ch6 at beg of round. (24 sets of 3tr)

Fasten off yarn.

MATERIALS

Rowan Felted Tweed DK (50% merino wool, 25% alpaca, 25% viscose; approx. 175m/191yd per 50g/1¾oz ball)

A shade 154 Ginger x 1 ball

B shade 151 Bilberry x 1 ball

C shade 152 Watery x 1 ball

D shade 157 Camel x 1 ball

E shade 183 Peony x 1 ball

F shade 150 Rage x 1 ball

G shade 184 Celadon x 1 ball

H shade 182 Damask x 1 ball

I shade 171 Paisley x 1 ball

J shade 173 Duck Egg x 1 ball

K shade 179 Horizon x 1 ball

EQUIPMENT

Crochet hook size 4mm (US G/6)
Sewing up needle

GAUGE

Approx. 4 rounds of pattern = 9cm (3½in)

FINISHED SIZE

Approx. 12.5cm x 12.5cm (5in x 5in)

SEE DIAGRAM PAGE 123

Work a further 8 motifs in the following
  colour scheme:

motif 2	motif 3	motif 4
Round 1: E	Round 1: G	Round 1: H
Round 2: A	Round 2: F	Round 2: I
Round 3: C	Round 3: E	Round 3: J
Round 4: F	Round 4 - 5: D	Round 4: C
Round 5: D		Round 5: D

motif 5	motif 6	motif 7
Round 1: I	Round 1: J	Round1 : B
Round 2: K	Round 2: A	Round 2: G
Rounds 3: B	Round 3: E	Round 3: A
Round 4-5: D	Round 4: G	Round 4 – 5: D
	Round 5: D	

motif 8	motif 9
Round 1: G	Round 1: C
Round 2: C	Round 2: J
Round 3: I	Round 3: F
Round 4: B	Round 4 – 5: D
Round 5: D	

ASSEMBLY

Weave in loose ends, then gently block
  and press to correct size.
Using yarn A, sew all the motifs together
  in one long strip.

FINISHING

Work a border of dc around the outer edge
  of the table runner as follows:
Using 4mm (US G/6) hook and yarn A join
  yarn into 1st st of long edge, ch1, 1dc into
  1st 3 sts, * 1dc into chsp, 1dc into next 3 sts,
  rep from * until you reach 1st corner, work
  3dc into ch3sp, repeat this process working
  1dc into each st, 1dc into ch1sp's and 3tr into
  ch3sp.

stacking pots

These mini stacking pots are perfect for parties and entertaining. Pack them full of candy and treats; no one will be able to resist!

INTERMEDIATE

PATTERN

large pot

Using yarn A (2 ends held together) and 5mm (US H/8) hook, ch2.

Round 1: 8sc into 2nd ch from hook, join with sl st into ch1 at beg of round. (8 sts)

Round 2: Ch1, 2dc into 1st st, 2dc into each st to end, join with sl st into ch1 at beg of round. (16 sts)

Round 3: Ch1, 1dc into 1st st, * 2dc into next st, 1dc into next st, rep from * to last st, 2dc into last st, join with sl st into ch1 at beg of round. (24 sts)

Round 4: Ch1, 1dc into 1st 2 sts, * 2dc into next st, 1dc into next 2 sts, rep from * to last st, 2dc into last st, join with sl st into ch1 at beg of round. (32 sts)

Round 5: Ch1, 1dc into 1st 3 sts, * 2dc into next st, 1dc into next 3 sts, rep from * to last st, 2dc into last st, join with sl st into ch1 at beg of round. (40 sts)

Round 6: Ch1, 1dc into 1st 4 sts, * 2dc into next st, 1dc into next 4 sts, rep from * to last st, 2dc into last st, join with sl st into ch1 at beg of round. (48 sts)

Round 7: Ch1, 1dc into each st to end, join with sl st into ch1 at beg of round.

Repeat round 7 another 10 times. Break off yarn.

medium pot

Using yarn B (2 ends held together) and 5mm (US H/8) hook, work rounds 1–5 as given for Large Pot then continue as follows:

Round 6: Ch1, 1dc into each st to end; join with sl st into ch1 at beg of round.

Repeat round 6 another 10 times. Break off yarn.

small pot

Using yarn C (2 ends held together) and 5mm (US H/8) hook, work rounds 1–4 as given for Large Pot then continue as follows:

Round 5: Ch1, 1dc into each st to end, join with sl st into ch1 at beg of round.

Repeat round 5 another 10 times. Break off yarn.

FINISHING

Weave in loose ends.

MATERIALS

Mission Falls 136 Merino Superwash (100% merino wool; approx. 124m/136yd per 50g/1¾oz ball)

A shade 379 Squash x 1 ball

Brown Sheep Nature Spun Worsted (100% wool; approx 224m/245yd per 100g/3½oz ball)

B shade 0188 Snow x 1 ball

C shade 040 Turquoise Wonder x 1 ball

EQUIPMENT

Crochet hook size 5mm (US H/8)

GAUGE

Approx. 15 sts x 20 rows = 10cm (4in) in double crochet with yarn held double

FINISHED SIZE

Large: approx. 9cm (3½in) wide and 6.5cm (2½in) deep

Medium: approx. 8cm (3in) wide and 6.5cm (2½in) deep

Small: approx. 7cm (2¾in) wide and 6.5cm (2½in) deep

bunny egg cosy

tip

Use the basic pattern as the base
of your own animal-inspired cosy.

Keep your boiled eggs nice and warm with these
character-based egg cosies. The bunny is worked from
the top down and the owl from the bottom up, but both
on the round so minimal sewing is required.

PATTERN

body

Using yarn A and D/3 hook, ch2.

Round 1: 6dc into 2nd ch from hook,
sl st into ch1 at beg of round. (6 sts)

Round 2: Ch1, 2dc into 1st st, 2dc
into each st to end, sl st into ch1 at
beg of round. (12 sts)

Round 3: Ch1, 1dc into each st to end,
sl st into ch1 at beg of round.

Round 4: Ch1, 1dc into 1st st, * 2dc
into next st, 1dc into next st, rep
from * to last st, 2dc into last st,
sl st into ch1 at beg of round.
(18 sts)

Round 5: As round 3.

Round 6: Ch1, 1dc into 1st 2 sts, * 2dc
into next st, 1dc into next 2 sts, rep
from * to last st, 2dc into last st, sl
st into ch1 at beg of round. (24 sts)

Round 7: As round 3.

Round 8: Ch1, 1dc into 1st 3 sts, * 2dc
into next st, 1dc into next 3 sts, rep
from * to last st, 2dc into last st,
sl st into ch1 at beg of round.
(30 sts)

Rounds 9 – 13: As round 3.

Rounds 14 – 18: Ch1, 1dc into back
loop of 1st st, 1dc into back loop
of each st to end, sl st into ch1 at
beg of round.

Break off yarn.

ears (make 2)

Using yarn A and 3mm (US D/3)
hook, ch4 + 1 turning chain.

Row 1: 1dc into 2nd ch from hook, 1dc
into each ch to end, turn. (4 sts)

Row 2: ch1, 1dc into each st to end.

Repeat row 2 a further 6 times.

Shape top as follows: Miss 1st st, *
work (2htr, 2tr) into next st, rep
from * once more, miss top of
last st, sl st into side of st.

Break off yarn.

Using yarn B, make a pom pom
approx. 4cm (1½in) wide.

ASSEMBLY

Gently block and press ears, then
stitch to 5th round making sure
sl st is to the centre of the back.

Attach pom pom to centre back using
sl st marks as a guide just above 1st
row of back loop tr.

FINISHING

Using picture as a guide, sew shirt
buttons to front for eyes.

Embroider pink nose in between eyes
using satin stitch and sew mouth
using black thread.

owl egg cosy

PATTERN

Using 3mm (US D/3) hook, ch32, join ends together to form a loop, making sure the chain is not twisted.

Round 1: Ch1, 1dc into each ch to end, join with sl st into ch1 at beg of round.

Round 2: Ch1, 1dc into back loop of next and each dc to end, join with sl st into ch1 at beg of round.

Repeat round 2 a further 4 times.

Round 7: Ch1, 1dc into 1st st, 1dc into each st to end, join with sl st into ch1 at beg of round.

Repeat round 7 a further 5 times.

Next round (shape top): Ch1, 1dc into 1st 2 sts, * 2dctog over next 2 sts, 1dc into next 2 sts, rep from * to last 2 sts, 2dctog over last 2 sts, join with sl st into ch1 at beg of round. (24 sts)

Next round: Ch1, 1dc into 1st st, 1dc into next st to end, sl st into ch1 at beg of round.

Next round: Ch1, 1dc into next 4 sts, 1htr into next st, 1tr into next 2 sts, 1tr into next st, 1dc into next 8 sts, 1htr into next st, 1tr into next 2 sts, 1htr into next st, 1dc into each st to end, sl st into ch1 at beg of round. Break yarn and secure.

ASSEMBLY

Sew along open top seam, making sure that the sl st join is to the centre back of work and the ears match up.

FINISHING

Cut 2 felt circles approx. 1.25cm (½in) wide, stitch onto front of owl using picture as guide.

Stitch shirt buttons towards the bottom of the felt fabric.

Stitch a small 'V' in between eyes.

Weave in loose ends.

MATERIALS

Rowan Fine Tweed (100% wool; approx. 90m/98yd per 25g/1oz ball), shade 373 Dent x 1 ball

Mustard yellow felt fabric for eyes, with thread to match

Shirt buttons x 2

Black thread

Orange embroidery thread for beak

EQUIPMENT

Crochet hook size 3mm (US D/3)

GAUGE

Approx. 25 sts x 25 rows = 10cm (4in) in double crochet

FINISHED SIZE

Approx. 7cm x 7cm (2¾in x 2¾in)

trivet

This trivet is an interesting take on the traditional square and is perfect for practicing crochet in the round and understanding how corners work. You can sew two together to make the design thicker and more robust.

PATTERN

Using yarn A and 3mm (US D/3) hook, ch6, join ends together with sl st to form a ring.

Round 1: Ch3 (counts as 1tr), 2tr into ring, * ch2, 3tr into ring, rep from * twice more, 3tr into ring, sl st into top of ch3 at beg of round. (12 sts)

Round 2: Ch3 (counts as 1tr), 1tr into next 2 sts, * work (2tr, ch2, 2tr) into ch2sp (1st corner worked), 1tr into next 3 sts, rep from * twice more, work (2tr, ch2, 2tr) into last ch2sp, sl st into top ch3 at beg of round. (28 sts)

Round 3: Ch3 (counts as 1tr), 1tr into next 4 sts, * work (2tr, ch2, 2tr) into ch2sp (1st corner worked), 1tr into next 7 sts, rep from * twice more, work (2tr, ch2, 2tr) into last ch2sp,1tr into last 2 sts, sl st into top ch3 at beg of round. (44 sts)

Round 4: Ch3 (counts as 1tr), 1tr into next 6 sts, * work (2tr, ch2, 2tr) into ch2sp (1st corner worked), 1tr into next 11 sts, rep from * twice more, work (2tr, ch2, 2tr) into last ch2sp, 1tr into last 4 sts, sl st into top ch3 at beg of round. (60 sts)

Break off yarn.

EDGING

With wrong side facing, join in yarn B at one of the ch2sps.

Row 1: Ch3 (counts as 1tr), 1tr into each st to ch2sp, work (2tr, ch2, 2tr) into ch2sp, 1tr into each st to next ch2sp, 1tr into ch2sp, turn. (35 sts)

Row 2: Ch3 (counts as 1tr), miss 1st st, 1tr into each st to ch2sp, work (2tr, ch2, 2tr) into ch2sp, 1tr into each st to next ch2sp, 1tr into ch2sp, turn. (39 sts)

Repeat row 2 another 4 times.

Fasten off yarn.

FINISHING

Make hanging loop as follows: using 3mm (US size D/3) hook and yarn B, insert hook into ch2sp opposite colour block and attach yarn. Ch30 then sl st into same ch2sp to form hanging loop.

For longer loop work extra chains.

MATERIALS

Rowan Cotton Glacé (100% cotton; approx. 115m/125yd per 50g/1¾oz ball)

A shade 828 Heather x 1 ball

B shade 739 Dijon x 1 ball

EQUIPMENT

Crochet hook size 3mm (US D/3)

GAUGE

Approx. 19 sts x 10 rows over 10cm (4in) in double crochet

FINISHED SIZE

Approx. 15cm x 15cm (6in x 6in)

heart motif bag

Give your canvas tote a makeover with these super-simple heart motifs. Go for a classic colour combination of pinks and reds, then scatter and stitch onto the ready-made bag.

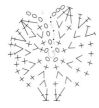

SEE DIAGRAM PAGE 123

projects

PATTERN

Make 9 motifs in total: 2 in A, B, D and E and 1 in C, or play with colours for your own variation.

Using yarn A and 3mm (US D/3) hook, ch4 and join with sl st to form ring.

Round 1: Ch2, work 8dc into 2nd ch from hook, join with sl st into 1ch at beg of round. (8 sts)

Round 2: Ch1, 2dc into each st to end, join with sl st into 1ch beg of round. (16 sts)

Round 3: Ch1 , 1dc into 1st st, 2dc into next st, * 1dc into next st, 2dc into next st, rep from * to end, join with sl st into 1ch at beg of round. (24 sts)

Round 4: Ch3, 3trtog over 1st 3 sts, 2tr into next st, 2htr into next st, 1dc into next 5 sts, (2trtog over next 2 sts) twice, 1dc into next 5 sts, 2htr into next st, 2tr into next st, 3trtog over last 3 sts, ch3, sl st into sl st from prev round.

Fasten off yarn.

ASSEMBLY

Weave in loose ends, then gently block and press.

Using picture as a guide, pin hearts onto bag. Sew motifs down their centre onto the bag using back stitch.

MATERIALS

Rowan Cotton Glacé (100% cotton; approx. 115m/125yd per 50g/1¾oz ball)

A shade 845 Shell x 1 ball

B shade 724 Bubbles x 1 ball

C shade 741 Poppy x 1 ball

Rowan Siena 4 ply (100% cotton; approx. 140m/153yd per 1¾oz/50g ball)

D shade 680 Lipstick x 1 ball

E shade 666 Chili x 1 ball

Canvas shopping bag x 1

EQUIPMENT

Crochet hook size 3mm (US D/3)

Pins

Sewing needle and thread

GAUGE

Not crucial

FINISHED SIZE

Approx. 4cm (1½in) per motif

large heart neck purse

This is the perfect party bag! Crocheted in the round, from the bottom up, with increasing and decreasing to make the fantastic heart-shape top. The neck strap is made from a twisted cord, but a fancy ribbon or simple crochet chain would work just as well.

PATTERN

Using 4mm (US G/6) hook, ch2.

Round 1: 6dc into 2nd ch from hook, join with sl st into ch1 at beg of round. (6 sts)

Round 2: Ch1, 1dc into 1st st, * 2dc into next st, 1dc into next st, rep from * to last st, 2dc into last st, join with sl st into ch1 at beg of round. (9 sts)

Round 3: Ch1, 1dc into each st to end, join with sl st into ch1 at beg of round.

Round 4: Ch1, 1dc into 1st 2 sts, * 2dc into next st, 1dc into next 2 sts, rep from * to last st, 2dc into last st, join with sl st into ch1 at beg of round. (12 sts)

Round 5: As round 3.

Round 6: Ch1, 1dc into 1st 3 sts, * 2dc into next st, 1dc into next 3 sts, rep from * to last st, 2dc into last st, join with sl st into ch1 at beg of round. (15 sts)

Round 7: As round 3.

Round 8: Ch1, 1dc into 1st 4 sts, * 2dc into next st, 1dc into next 4 sts, rep from * to last st, 2dc into last st, join with sl st into ch1 at beg of round. (18 sts)

Round 9: As round 3.

Round 10: Ch1, 1dc into 1st 5 sts, * 2dc into next st, 1dc into next 5 sts, rep from * to last st, 2dc into last st, join with sl st into ch1 at beg of round. (21 sts)

Round 11: Ch1, 1dc into 1st 6 sts, * 2dc into next st, 1dc into next 6 sts, rep from * to last st, 2dc into last st, join with sl st into ch1 at beg of round. (24 sts)

Round 12: Ch1, 1dc into 1st 7 sts, * 2dc into next st, 1dc into next 7 sts, rep from * to last st, 2dc into last st, join with sl st into ch1 at beg of round. (27 sts)

Round 13: Ch1, 1tr into 1st 8 sts, * 2dc into next st, 1dc into next 8 sts, rep from * to last st, 2dc into last st, join with sl st into ch1 at beg of round. (30 sts)

Round 14: Ch1, 1dc into 1st 9 sts, * 2dc into next st, 1dc into next 9 sts, rep from * to last st, 2dc into last st, join with sl st into ch1 at beg of round. (33 sts)

Round 15: As round 3.

Round 16: Ch1, 1dc into 1st 10 sts, * 2dc into next st, 1dc into next 10 sts, rep from * to last st, 2dc into last st, join with sl st into ch1 at beg of round. (36 sts)

MATERIALS

Rowan Creative Focus Worsted (75% wool, 25% alpaca; approx. 200m/220yd per 100g/3½oz ball), shade 2055 Carmine x 1 ball

EQUIPMENT

Crochet hook size 4mm (US G/6)

Sewing up needle

GAUGE

Approx. 18 sts x 20 rows = 10cm (4in) in double crochet

FINISHED SIZE

Approx. 10cm (4in) wide, 11.5cm (4½in) deep

Rounds 17 – 18: As round 3.

Shape top of heart as follows over next 18 sts only:

Rows 1 – 3: Ch1, 1dc into each of the next 18 sts, turn.

Row 4: Ch1, (1dc into next st, 2dctog over next 2 sts, 1dc into next 3 sts, 2dctog over next 2 sts, 1dc into next st) twice, turn. (14 sts)

Row 5: Ch1, 1dc into each st to end, turn.

Row 6: Ch1, (1dc into 1st st, * 2dctog over next 2 sts, 1dc into next st, rep from * once more) twice, turn. (10 sts)

Row 7: Ch2, (5trtog over next 5 sts) twice, ch2, sl st into base of tr.

Break off yarn.

Rejoin yarn to main fabric and repeat rows 1–7.

ASSEMBLY

Weave in loose ends, then gently block and press.

Using approx. 47 in (120 cm) of yarn, make a twisted cord or alternatively use ribbon. Thread sewing up needle with non-knotted end of twisted cord, bring needle up through left-hand top of heart and back down through right-hand top of heart. Knot the open end to secure.

rolled wrist band

Say it with accessories! Dress up your outfit with this floral wrist corsage, worked as a strip with a shell stitch edge then rolled up to make a flower shape. Why not add beads or buttons to the centre for sparkle or try adding a crochet leaf?

PATTERN

Using 4mm (US G/6) hook, ch15 + 1 turning ch.

Row 1: 1dc into 2nd ch from hook, 1dc into each ch to end, turn. (15 sts)

Row 2: Ch1, 2dc into 1st st, 2dc into each st to end, turn. (30 sts)

Row 3: As row 2. (60 sts)

Row 4: Ch1, miss 1st st, 5tr into next st, miss 1, 1dc into next st, (miss next st, 5tr into next st, dc into next st) 3 times (miss 2, 7tr into next st, miss 2, 1dc into next st) 7 times.

Fasten off yarn.

ASSEMBLY

Weave in loose ends and roll up strip to form a flower shape and hold together with safety pin.

Sew the flower together at the base, making sure you go through all the layers.

Next cut elastic to required length, making sure the ends overlap by approx. 1cm (½in) and sew the elastic together to form the band. Sew the flower onto the spot where the band has been stitched together to cover the join.

MATERIALS
Rowan Creative Focus Worsted (75% wool, 25% alpaca; approx. 200m/220yd per 100g/3½oz ball), shade 1890 Magenta x 1 ball

1.25cm (½in) wide elastic, 20cm (8in) length

Thread to match elastic

EQUIPMENT
Crochet hook size 4mm (US G/6)

Sharp sewing needle

Sewing up needle

Large safety pin

GAUGE
Approx. 18 sts x 20 rows = 10cm (4in) in double crochet

FINISHED SIZE
Approx. 6cm (2¼in) wide

lipstick case

This design is perfect for keeping your favourite lipstick at hand. The main fabric is worked in a textured stitch and the ends are simple, circular discs. Stitch the pieces together and close with snaps.

PATTERN

Using 3mm (US D/3) hook, ch21 + 1 turning ch.

Row 1: 1dc into 2nd ch from hook, 1dc into each ch to end. (20 sts)

Row 2: Ch1, (1htr, 1tr) into next st, * miss 2, (1dc, 1htr, 1tr) into next st, rep from * to last 3 sts, miss 2, 1dc into last st, turn.

Repeat row 2 another 15 times.

Break off yarn.

ends (make 2)

Using 3mm (US D/3) hook, make a magic circle.

Round 1: 8dc into magic circle then pull tight to close circle, sl st into ch1 at beg of round.

Round 2: Ch1, 2dc into each st. (16 sts)

ASSEMBLY

Weave in loose ends, then gently block and press pieces.

Using safety pins, pin the circles to the longer outer edges, allowing the main fabric to overlap forming the flap. Sew circles into position.

Sew snaps to the main fabric.

MATERIALS

Rowan Cotton Glacé (100% cotton; approx. 115m/125yd per 50g/1¾oz ball), shade 724 Bubbles x 1 ball

Snaps for fastening x 2

Black sewing cotton

EQUIPMENT

Crochet hook size 3mm (US D/3)

Sharp sewing needle

Safety pins x 2

GAUGE

Approx. 21 sts x 13 rows = 10cm (4in) in pattern

FINISHED SIZE

Approx. 10cm x 11.5cm (4in x 4½in)

flower key chain

Show off your crochet skills with this fancy floral key ring. Worked in the round, this design is good for practising colour changes.

PATTERN

Using yarn A and 3mm (US D/3) hook, ch4 and join ends together with sl st to form a ring.

Round 1: Ch1, 8dc into ring, join with sl st into ch1 at beg of round. (8 sts)

Break off yarn A and join in yarn B.

Round 2: Ch1, 2dc into 1st st, 2dc into each st to end, join with sl st into ch1 at beg of round. (16 sts)

Break off yarn B and join in yarn C.

Round 3: Ch2, work 4trtog over next 4 sts, ch2, sl st into same st as last tr worked (first petal worked), * sl st into next st, ch2, work 4trtog over 4 sts, start 1st tr by inserting hook into same place as last sl st just worked, ch2, sl st into same st as last tr worked, rep from * to end. (5 petals)

This round is worked at back of work.

Round 4: Working into the back loop of all sts, sl st into next 2 sts, * work ch3, miss next 4 sts, sl st into back of next st, rep from * ending last rep with sl st into 1st ch3sp. (5 loops)

Work next round into the ch3 spaces at back of work.

Round 5: Working into the ch3 spaces at back of work, ch1, 1dc into ch3sp, (ch3, 4quad trtog, ch3, 1dc) into same ch3sp, * (1dc, ch3, 4quad trtog, ch3, 1dc) into next ch3sp, rep from * to end, sl st into ch1 at beg of round. (5 petals)

Break off yarn.

ASSEMBLY

Attach key ring clip as follows:
Using yarn C and 3mm (US D/3) hook, ch20.

Break off yarn.

Slip key ring clip onto chain and attach chain to back of flower.

FINISHING

Weave in loose ends, gently press and block flower.

MATERIALS

Patons Cotton DK (100% cotton; approx. 210m/ 230yd per 100g/3½oz ball)

A shade 2729 Delta x 1 ball

B shade 2743 Purple x 1 ball

C shade 2738 Garnet x 1 ball

Key chain

EQUIPMENT

Crochet hook size 3mm (US D/3)

GAUGE

Not crucial

FINISHED SIZE

Approx. 5.5cm (2in) wide

hexagon motif purse

Crochet motifs are a bit like building blocks. This design uses simple hexagons joined together to create a flap-top purse. Make the design larger by simply adding more motifs.

PATTERN

small motif (make 10)

Using yarn A and 4mm (US G/6), ch6, join with sl st to form ring.

Round 1: Ch3 (counts as 1tr), 2trtog into ring, * ch3, 3trtog into ring, rep from * 4 more times, ch3, sl st into top of ch3 at beg of round.

Fasten off yarn A and join in yarn B.

Round 2: Sl st into 1st ch3sp, ch3 (counts as 1tr), (2tr, ch2, 3tr) into same sp, *(3tr, ch2, 3tr) into next ch3sp, rep from * to end, sl st into top of ch3 at beg of round.

Fasten off yarn B and join in yarn C.

Round 3: Ch1, 1dc into each st to 1st ch2sp, * 2dc into ch2sp, 1dc into each st up to next ch2sp, rep from * to last ch2sp, 1dc into each st to end.

top flap (large motif)

Continue with yarn A, ch6, join with sl st to form ring.

Round 1: Ch3 (counts as 1tr), 2trtog into ring, * ch3, 3trtog into ring, rep from * 4 more times, ch3, sl st into top of ch3 at beg of round.

Fasten off yarn A and join in yarn D.

Round 2: Sl st into 1st ch3sp, ch3 (counts as 1tr), (2trtog, ch2, 3trtog) into same sp, * (3trtog, ch2, 3trtog) into next ch3sp, rep from * to end, sl st into top of ch3 at beg of round.

Fasten off yarn D and join in yarn B.

Round 3: Sl st into 1st ch2sp, ch3 (counts as 1tr), (2tr, ch2, 3tr) into same sp, * 3tr into next sp, **(3tr, ch2, 3tr) into next ch2sp, rep from * ending last rep at **, sl st into top of ch3 at beg of round. Fasten off yarn B and join in yarn C.

Round 4: Ch1, 1dc into each st to 1st ch2sp, * 2dc into ch2sp, 1dc into each st up to next ch2sp, rep from * to last ch2sp, 1dc into each st to end, sl st into ch1 at beg of round.

ASSEMBLY

Weave in loose ends, then block and press each motif to correct size, making sure each block has 6 straight sides.

Using picture as a guide, sew motifs together, then sew larger motif to the back section, making sure the front point of the flap sits at the top of the second row of motifs at the front.

Sew button into place.

SEE DIAGRAM PAGE 124

MATERIALS

Rowan Felted Tweed (50% merino wool, 25% alpaca, 25% viscose; approx. 175m/191yd per 50g/ 1¾oz ball)

A shade 173 Duck Egg Blue x 1 ball

B shade 177 Clay x 1 ball

C shade 150 Rage x 1 ball

D shade 170 Seafarer x 1 ball

EQUIPMENT

Crochet hook size 4mm (US G/6)

1 x 2.5cm (1in) wide button

GAUGE

Size of small motif approx. 6.5cm (2½in)

FINISHED SIZE

14cm x 15cm (5½in x 6in)

layered picot necklace

You can create this necklace with the most basic of crochet skills. The design is worked throughout using the double crochet stitch and chain with the addition of a picot, which adds a touch of texture and interest.

PATTERN

Using yarn A and 3mm (US D/3) hook, work first necklace strand as follows:

Row 1: Ch12, 1 sl st into 3rd ch from hook (1 picot worked), * 8ch–1 picot, rep from * 11 more times, 9ch, turn.

Row 2: Ch1, 1dc into 1st 6ch, ch6, 1 picot, * ch9, 1 picot, rep from * 11 times, ch3, 6dc into last ch6.

Break yarn A and join in B.

Row 3: Ch1, 1dc into 1st 6 sts,* ch10, 1 picot, rep from * 12 times, ch7, 1dc into last 6 sts, turn.

Row 4: Ch1, 1dc into 1st 6 sts, ch11, 1 picot, *ch11, 1 picot, rep from * 11 times, ch8, 1dc into last 6 sts.

Break yarn B and join in C.

Row 5: Ch1, 1dc into 1st 6 sts,* ch12, 1 picot, rep from * 12 times, ch9, 1dc into last 6 sts, turn.

Row 6: Ch1, 1dc into next 6dc, ch13, 1 picot, * ch13, 1 picot, rep from * 11 times, ch10, 1dc into last 6 sts.

FINISHING

Weave in loose ends.

Pin out the necklace on an ironing board or suitable surface, cover with a damp tea towel and gently press with a steam iron.

Leave to dry.

Make 2 button loops by working approx. 8ch for each, then sew button to match at the other side.

MATERIALS

Rowan Cotton Glacé (100% cotton; approx. 115m/125yd per 50g/1¾oz ball)

A shade 844 Green Slate x 1 ball

B shade 849 Windsor x 1 ball

C shade 850 Cobalt x 1 ball

Small shirt buttons x 2

EQUIPMENT

Crochet hook size 3mm (US D/3)

GAUGE

Not crucial

FINISHED SIZE

Top layer approx. 34cm (13½in), bottom layer approx. 52cm (20½in)

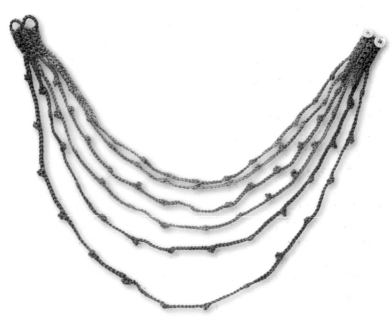

layered circular motif cushion

This project is a good introduction to working in the round. The circles are crocheted in contrast colours; mix it up or keep it tonal, either way it's a great way of adding a new twist to an existing cushion.

PATTERN

Large circle (make 9: 2 x A, B, C and E, 1 x D)

Using 3mm (US D/3) hook, ch2.

Round 1: 8dc into 2nd ch from hook, sl st into ch1 at beg of round. (8 sts)

Round 2: Ch1, 2dc into each st, sl st into ch1 at beg of round. (16 sts)

Round 3: Ch1, 1dc into 1st st, * 2dc into next st, 1dc into next st, rep from * to last st, 2dc into last st, sl st into ch1 at beg of round. (24 sts)

Round 4: Ch1, 1dc into 1st 2 sts, * 2dc into next st, 1dc into next 2 sts, rep from * to last st, 2dc into last st, sl st into ch1 at beg of round. (32 sts)

Break off yarn.

Small circle (make 9: 3 x A, 1 x B, 2 x C and D, 1 x E)

Using 3mm (US D/3) hook, ch2.

Round 1: 8dc into 2nd ch from hook, sl st into ch1 at beg of round. (8 sts)

Round 2: Ch1, 2dc into each st, sl st into ch1 at beg of round. (16 sts)

Break off yarn.

FINISHING

Weave in loose ends and gently block and press.

ASSEMBLY

Using picture as a guide, layer up the small and large circular motifs, stitch together using back stitch around the centre.

Place in a grid formation on the front of the cushion, then stitch the larger motif to the fabric.

MATERIALS

Rowan Cotton Glace (100% cotton; approx. 115m/125yd per 50g/1¾oz ball)

A shade 829 Twilight x 1 ball

B shade 739 Dijon x 1 ball

C shade 850 Cobalt x 1 ball

D shade 849 Windsor x 1 ball

E shade 858 Aqua x 1 ball

25cm (10in) square covered cushion pad x 1

EQUIPMENT

Crochet hook size 3mm (US D/3)

Sewing needle

GAUGE

Not crucial

FINISHED SIZE

Large circle: approx. 4cm (1½in)

Small circle: approx. 2.5cm (1in)

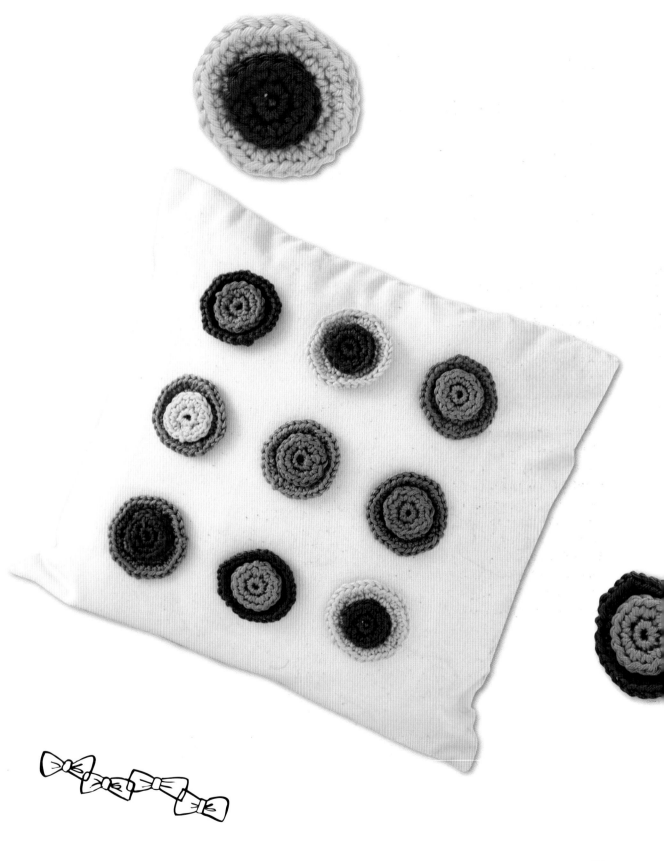

granny square slip cover

Bring the granny square right up-to-date with this tablet slipcover. The front and back panels are made up of small squares stitched together. The larger panels are then crocheted together, making sure there is enough space for your tablet to fit snugly.

PATTERN (MAKE 12)

Using yarn A and 4mm (US G/6) hook, ch 4 and join ends together with sl st to form ring.

Round 1: Ch6 (counts as 1tr and ch3), * 3tr into ring, ch3 rep from * twice more, 2tr into ring, join with sl st into 3rd of ch6 at beg of round. Sl st into 1st ch 3 sp.

Fasten off yarn A and join in yarn B.

Round 2: Ch6 (counts as 1tr and ch3), work 3tr into 1st ch3sp, * ch1, work (3tr, 3ch, 3tr) into next ch3sp, rep from * twice more, 2tr into 1st ch3sp, sl st 3rd of ch6 at beg of round. Sl st into ch3sp.

Fasten off yarn B and join in yarn C.

Round 3: Ch6 (counts as 1tr and ch3), work 3tr into 1st ch3sp, * ch1, 3tr into next ch1sp, work (3tr, 3ch, 3tr) into next ch3sp, rep from * twice more, ch1, 3tr into next ch1sp, 2tr into 1st ch3sp, sl st into 3rd of ch6 at beg of round. Sl st into ch3sp.

Fasten off yarn C.

Make 1 more motif as given above, then work a further 10 motifs, 2 in each colourway, according to the table opposite.

MATERIALS

Rowan Felted Tweed DK (50% merino wool, 25% alpaca, 25% viscose; approx. 175m/191yd per 50g/1¾oz ball)

A shade 150 Rage x 1 ball

B shade 161 Avocado x 1 ball

C shade 152 Watery x 1 ball

D shade 183 Peony x 1 ball

E shade 181 Mineral x 1 ball

EQUIPMENT

Crochet hooks sizes 4mm (US G/6) and 3mm (US D/3)

GAUGE

Approx. 6.5cm (2½in) square per motif

FINISHED SIZE

Approx. 12.5cm x 19cm (5in x 7½in)

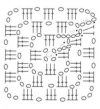

SEE DIAGRAM PAGE 122

motif 3&4	motif 5&6	motif 7&8
Round 1: B	Round 1: C	Round 1: D
Round 2: C	Round 2: E	Round 2: B
Round 3: D	Round 3: A	Round 3: E

motif 9&10	motif 11&12
Round 1: D	Round 1: E
Round 2: A	Round 2: D
Rounds 3: B	Round 3: C

ASSEMBLY

Weave in loose ends, then block and press each motif to
correct size.

Each panel is made up of 6 motifs. Using picture as a guide,
lay the motifs out 2 wide and 3 deep, then sew together
to form 1 large panel. Repeat with the remaining 6 motifs.

Crochet the 2 larger panels together leaving the top open as
zig-zagging between the front and back panels as follows:

Using 3mm (US D/3) hook join yarn A to the top left-hand
corner of front panel, ch1, sl st into top corner of back
panel, ch1, sl st into 1st st on front panel, ch1, sl st into 1st
st of back panel, * ch1, miss next st on front panel, sl st
into next st, ch1, miss next st on back panel, sl st into next
st, rep from * until you have worked around the panels
leaving the top open.

Weave in loose ends.

floral cushion motifs

Give an old cushion a new lease of life with this quick and easy project. It's a great way to use up all those odd bits 'n' bobs of yarn left over from other projects. The flower heads are worked in the round using double crochet and picot edging then stitched into position.

MATERIALS

Rowan Cotton Glacé (100% cotton; approx. 115m/125yd per 50g/1¾oz ball)

A shade 741 Poppy x 1 ball

B shade 841 Garnet x 1 ball

C shade 724 Bubbles x 1 ball

D shade 856 Mineral x 1 ball

E shade 832 Persimmon x 1 ball

F shade 726 Bleached x 1 ball

Small amount of yarn/ embroidery thread for stems in Lime/Slate/Turquoise

Small amount of felt fabric for leaf in Bottle/ Grasl st/Lime

25cm (10in) square covered cushion pad

Sewing thread

EQUIPMENT

Crochet hook size 3mm (US D/3)

Sewing needle

GAUGE

Approx. 30 sts x 25 rows = 10cm (4in) in double crochet

FINISHED SIZE

Large circle: approx. 4cm (1½in)

Small circle: approx. 2.5cm (1in)

COLOUR COMBINATIONS

Flower A (circle)	Round 1: A	Round 2: B	Rounds 3 – 4: C
Flower B (picot)	Round 1: C	Round 2: D	Rounds 3 – 4: E
Flower C (picot)	Round 1: E	Round 2: D	Rounds 3 – 4: F
Flower D (circle)	Round 1: B	Round 2: C	Rounds 3 – 4: D
Flower B (picot)	Rounds 1 – 2: A	Round 3: B	Rounds 4: C

PATTERN

Using 3mm (US D/3) hook and following the colour combinations given above, work in pattern as follows:

circular flower

Round 1: ch4 join ends together with sl st to form ring.

Round 2: ch1, 8sc into ring, sl st into ch1 at beg of round. (8 sts)

Round 3: ch1, 2sc into each st to end, sl st into ch1 at beg of round. (16 sts)

Round 4: ch1, *1sc into 1st st, 2sc into next st, rep from * to end, sl st into ch1 at beg of round. (24 sts)

Round 5: ch1, * 1sc into next 2 sts, 2sc into next st, rep from * to end, sl st into ch1 at beg of round. (32 sts)

picot edge flower

Work rounds 1 – 3 as given for circular
  flower and stripe combination and
  continue as follows: 1ch, * 1dc into
  next 2dc, (1dc, 3ch, sl sl into last dc
  just worked, 1dc) into next st, rep
  from * to end

Round 4: Ch1, * 1sc into next 2 sts,
  2sc into next st, make picot (MP) as
  follows 3ch then sl st back into last
  st just worked, rep from * to end, sl
  st into ch1 at beg of round. (32 sts)

FINISHING

Weave in loose ends and gently block
  and press.

ASSEMBLY

Place flowers on the cushion cover
  in the required position, using the
  picture as a guide, and sew into
  place using a sharp sewing needle
  and sewing thread.

Embroider the stem onto the cushion
  cover fabric using back stitch.

Cut the leaves out from the felt fabric
  and stitch into position.

picture frame

This crochet picture frame is designed to fit snugly around a standard size photograph or frame. The main part is worked first and shaped using increasing and decreasing techniques. Add the fancy trim afterwards – try using a contrast colour for a different look.

projects

PATTERN

Using 4mm (US H/8) hook, ch80 + 1 turning ch.

Row 1: 1dc into 1st 7 sts, 3dc into next ch, 1dc into next 24ch, 3dc into next ch, 1dc into next 14ch, 3dc into next ch, 1dc into next 24ch, 3dc into next ch, 1dc into last 7ch, turn. (88 sts)

Row 2: Ch1, 1dc into next 8 sts, 3dc into next st, 1dc into next 26 sts, 1dc into next st, 1dc into next 16 sts, 1dc into next st, 1dc into next 26 sts, 1dc into next st, 1dc last 8 sts, turn. (96 sts)

Row 3: Ch1, 1dc into next 9 sts, 3dc into next st, 1dc into next 28 sts, 1dc into next st, 1dc into next 18 sts, 1dc into next st, 1dc into next 28 sts, 1dc into next st, 1dc last 9 sts, turn. (104 sts)

Row 4: Working into back loop of each st, ch1, 1dc into next 9 sts, 3dctog over next 3 sts, 1dc into next 28 sts, 3dctog over next 3 sts, 1dc into next 18 sts, 3dctog over next 3 sts, 1dc into next 28 sts, 3dctog over next 3 sts, 1dc into last 9 sts, turn. (96 sts)

Row 5: Ch1, 1dc into next 8 sts, 3dctog over next 3 sts, 1dc into next 26 sts, 3dctog over next 3 sts, 1dc into next 16 sts, 3dctog over next 3 sts, 1dc into next 26 sts, 3dctog over next 3 sts, 1dc into last 8 sts, turn. (88 sts)

Row 6: Ch1, 1dc into next 7 sts, 3dctog over next 3 sts, 1dc into next 24 sts, 3dctog over next 3 sts, 1dc into next 14 sts, 3dctog over next 3 sts, 1dc into next 24 sts, 3dctog over next 3 sts, 1dc into last 7 sts, turn. (80 sts)

Break yarn and fasten off.

ASSEMBLY

Sew ends together and work fancy edging into the loops left from row 4 as follows:

Rejoin yarn at seam, inserting hook under loop and drawing yarn through, work 1sl st to secure and work trim: Miss 1, * work 1htr, 3tr, 1htr into next loop, miss 1, sl st into next loop, miss 1, rep from * ending last rep with sl st into base of htr at beg of round.

FINISHING

Weave in loose ends, then gently block and press the fancy outer edge trim.

covered coat hanger

This is a wardrobe update of a different kind. Add a touch of crochet to your coat hangers with this fabric worked in double crochet throughout then wrapped around the hanger and stitched into place.

MATERIALS

Rowan Cotton Glacé (100% cotton; approx. 115m/125yd per 50g/1¾oz ball)

A shade 850 Cobalt

B shade 741 Poppy

C shade 726 Bleached

EQUIPMENT

Crochet hook size 5mm (US H/8)

Padded coat hanger x 1

Sewing up needle

GAUGE

Approx. 14 sts x 15 rows = 10cm (4in) in double crochet with yarn held double

FINISHED SIZE

Approx. 40.5cm x 11.5cm (16in x 4½in)

PATTERN

Using 2 ends together throughout and yarn A and 5mm (US H/8) hook, ch13 + 1 turning ch.

Row 1: 1dc into 2nd ch from hook, turn. (13 sts)

Row 2: Ch1, 1dc into each st to end, turn.

Work all following rows as row 2 in the following stripe sequence:

Rows 3–10: Yarn A.

Rows 11–12: Yarn B.

Rows 13–14: Yarn C

Repeat rows 11–14 once more.

Rows 19–20: Yarn B.

Rows 21–39: Yarn A.

Rows 40–41: Yarn B.

Rows 42–43: Yarn C.

Repeat rows 40–43 once more.

Rows 48–49: Yarn B.

Rows 50–59: Yarn A.

Fasten off yarn.

ASSEMBLY

Weave in loose ends, then gently block and press to correct size.

Wrap the fabric around the coat hanger as follows: Find the centre point of the fabric and slip the fabric down onto the coat hanger at this point.

Sew the ends of the fabric together then sew along the open edge to cover the coat hanger.

card pouch

Keep your cards in one place with this handy little pouch. With its deep flap and elastic fastening, the cards will be nice and secure.

PATTERN

Using yarn A and 3mm (US D/3) hook, ch16 + 1 turning ch.

Row 1: 1dc into 2nd ch from hook, 1dc into each ch to end, turn. (16 sts)

Row 2: Ch1, 1dc into each st to end.

Break yarn A and join in yarn B.

Rows 3 – 4: As row 2.

Rows 1 – 4 form stripe pattern. Repeat these 4 rows a further 9 times.

Fasten off yarn.

ASSEMBLY

Weave in loose ends then block and press.

Fold strip of fabric into 3 even sections of approx. 14 rows per section, and sew up the side seams to form an envelope.

Thread elastic through button and feed ends of the elastic down through the centre front of the top panel, knot the ends and wrap around the outside and over the button to secure it in place.

You can also secure the elastic with a few stitches on the underside if required.

MATERIALS

Rowan Cotton Glacé (100% cotton; approx. 115m/125yd per 50g/1¾oz ball)

A shade 858 Aqua x 1 ball

B shade 829 Twilight x 1 ball

2cm (¾in) wide square button x 1

Elastic cord, 28cm (11in) length

EQUIPMENT

Crochet hook size 3mm (US D/3)

GAUGE

Approx. 20 sts x 22 rows = 10cm (4in) in double crochet

FINISHED SIZE

Approx. 9cm x 18cm (3½in x 7in)

luggage tag

Keep an eye on your luggage with this plaid tag. Crochet the stripes then add embellishments to create the plaid effect. The back has a plain panel that you can slip your contact details into.

PATTERN

front

Using yarn A and 3mm (US D/3) hook, ch14 + 1 turning ch.

Row 1: 1dc into 2nd ch from hook, 1dc into each ch to end, turn. (14 sts)

Row 2: Ch1, 1dc into each st to end.

Repeat row 2 in following stripe sequence:

Rows 3–4: Yarn A.

Rows 5–7: Yarn B.

Rows 8–11: Yarn A.

Rows 12–14: Yarn C.

Rows 15–18: Yarn A.

Rows 19–21: Yarn D.

Rows 22–23: Yarn A.

Next row (shape top): Ch1, 1dc into 1st st, 2dctog over next 2 sts, 1dc to last 3 sts, 2dctog over next 2 sts, 1dc into last st. (12 sts)

Next row: Ch1, 1dc into 1st st, 2dctog over next 2 sts, 1dc into next 2 sts, ch2, miss 2, 1dc into next 2 sts, 2dctog over next 2 sts, 1dc into last st. (10 sts)

Next row: Ch1, 1dc into 1st st, 2dctog over next 2 sts, 1dc into next st, 2dc into ch2sp, 1dc into next st, 2dctog over next 2 sts, 1dc into last st. (8 sts)

back

Using yarn A and 3mm (US D/3) hook, ch14 + 1 turning ch.

Row 1: 1dc into 2nd ch from hook, 1dc into each ch to end, turn. (14 sts)

Row 2: Ch1, 1dc into each st to end.

Repeat row 2 a further 19 times.

FINISHING

Using picture as a guide, work a contrast chain across the centre of each stripe on the front panel, a red stripe 4 sts in from left-hand side and a black stripe approx. 6 sts in from left-hand side, then work a white stripe across the top green stripe.

Weave in loose ends.

ASSEMBLY

Block and press front and back panels.

Pin back panel into position to the wrong side of the front panel, and sew around the edges leaving top open for your contact details.

Knot the ends of the elastic cord together to make a loop, then thread through ch2sp at top of front panel.

MATERIALS

Rowan Cotton Glacé (100% cotton; approx. 115m/125yd per 50g/1¾oz ball)

A shade 739 Dijon x 1 ball

B shade 741 Poppy x 1 ball

C shade 849 Windsor x 1 ball

D shade 856 Mineral x 1 ball

Small amount of black and white yarn for embroidery

Sewing thread

Cord elastic, 20cm (8in) length

EQUIPMENT

Crochet hook size 3mm (US D/3)

Large-eye embroidery needle

Sharp sewing needle

GAUGE

Approx. 20 sts x 22 rows = 10cm (4in) in double crochet

FINISHED SIZE

Approx. 6.5cm x 12cm (2½in x 4¾in)

chalk bag

No yarn nearby? Why not make your own by cutting old T shirts into strips. This recycled yarn will make a sturdy container for heavy objects such as climbing chalk.

MATERIALS

Recycled t-shirt fabric, approx. 3 adult t-shirts cut into 4cm (1½in) strips

Fat quarter of fabric for lining x 1

Thread to match fabric

Spring toggle x 1

Elastic cord, 40.5cm (16in) length

EQUIPMENT

Crochet hook size 9mm (US M/13)

Sharp sewing needle

GAUGE

Approx. 8 sts x 8 rows = 10cm (4in) in double crochet over

FINISHED SIZE

Approx. 14cm (5½in) deep, 30cm (12in) circumference

PATTERN

Using 9mm (US M/13) hook and yarn, ch2.

Round 1: 6dc into 2nd ch from hook, sl st into ch1 at beg of round. (6 sts)

Round 2: Ch1, 2dc into each st to end, sl st into ch1 at beg of round. (12 sts)

Round 3: Ch1, 1dc into 1st st, * 2dc into next st, 1dc into next st, rep from * to last st, 2dc into last st, sl st into ch1 at beg of round. (18 sts)

Round 4: Ch1, 1dc into 1st 2 sts, * 2dc into next st, 1dc into next 2 sts, rep from * to last st, 2dc into last st, sl st into ch1 at beg of round. (24 sts)

Round 5: Ch1, work 1dc around the stem of each stitch instead of into top of stitch to end, sl st into ch1 at beg of round.

Round 6: Ch1, 1dc into each st to end, sl st into ch1 at beg of round.

Repeat round 6 a further 10 times.

Break off yarn.

TAB

Using 9mm (US M/13) hook rejoin yarn to last round and work 1dc into the next 3 sts, turn. (3 sts)

Work 3 more rows in the same way.

Break yarn.

ASSEMBLY

Fold tab in half towards the inside of the pot and sew into place.

Weave in loose ends.

Make lining as follows: Cut length of fabric approx. 35cm (14in) wide and 19cm (7½in) deep. Cut a circle for base approx. 2.5cm (1in) wider than base.

Allow a 2.5cm (1in) seam allowance, pin and stitch the side seams of the longer length to form a tube.

Cut tabs into the circular base approx. 2cm (¾in) deep and approx. 1.25cm (½in) apart, to allow the base to sit flat.

Again allowing a 2.5cm (1in) seam allowance, pin and stitch the circular base to the bottom of the tube, making sure the right side of the fabric is to the inside of the tube.

Attach elastic pull cord as follows: Thread sewing up needle with elastic cord, insert needle approx. 2 rounds down from top opening and opposite tab, bring the needle back around on the inside to the same place forming a loop and bring the needle back out. Slip elastic through spring clip and knot the ends together to secure.

Place the fabric into the pot, fold over the top to form a seam, then stitch into place.

basic phone case

These mobile phone slipcover projects are a good way to expand your crochet knowledge. Choose from a simple double crochet stripe or more advanced fan stitch design to work in the round and build up. Both designs are finished off with a button and loop fastening.

PATTERN

Using yarn A and 4mm (US G/6) hook, ch11 + 1 turning chain.

Round 1: 1dc into 2nd ch from hook, 1dc into next 9ch, 3dc into last ch, then work back along chain as follows, 1dc into each of the next 9ch, 2dc into last ch, sl st into ch1 at beg of round. (24 sts)

Round 2: Ch1, 1dc into each st to end, sl st into ch1 at beg of round.

Repeat round 2 a further 13 times.

Break off yarn A and join in yarn B.

Rounds 16–17: As round 2.

Break off yarn B and join in yarn C.

Rounds 18–19: As round 2.

Rounds 16–19 form stripe pattern. Repeat these 4 rounds once more, then rounds 16–17 once more.

Break off yarn.

FINISHING

Weave in loose ends, block and press gently.

Make button loop as follows: Using 4mm (US G/6) hook and yarn C, insert hook into centre stitch of back panel of case and work ch16, sl st into same chain to close loop.

Weave in loose ends, sew button to centre of front panel matching up with button loop.

MATERIALS

Rowan Creative Focus Worsted (75% wool, 25% alpaca; approx. 200m/220yd per 100g/3½oz ball)

A shade 2755 Deep Rose x 1 ball

C shade 2055 Carmine x 1 ball

Rowan Felted Tweed Aran (50% merino, 25% alpaca, 25% viscose; approx. 87m/95yd per 50g/1¾oz ball)

B shade 720 Pebble x 1 ball

Button x 1

EQUIPMENT

Crochet hook size 4mm (US G/6)

GAUGE

Approx. 18 sts x 20 rows = 10cm (4in) in double crochet

FINISHED SIZE

Approx. 8cm x 12.5cm (3in x 5in)

advanced phone case

PATTERN

Using 4mm (US G/6) hook, ch11 + 1 turning chain.

Round 1: 1dc into 2nd ch from hook, 1dc into next 9ch, 3dc into last ch, then work back along chain as follows, 1dc into each of the next 9ch, 2dc into last ch, sl st into ch1 at beg of round. (24 sts) Round 2: Ch1, 1dc into 1st st, * miss 2, 5tr into next st, miss 2, 1dc into next st, rep from * ending last rep after 5tr's have been worked, sl st into ch1 at beg of round. (4 fans)

Round 3: Ch3 (counts as 1tr), 2trtog over 1st 2 sts, ch3, * sl st into next st, ch3, 5trtog over next 5 sts, ch3, 1dc into next st, rep from * twice more, ch3, 2trtog over last 2 sts, join with sl st into top of ch3 at beg of round.

Round 4: Ch3 (counts as 1tr), 2tr into 1st st, miss ch3, 1dc into next st, * 5tr into centre of 5trtog from prev round, miss ch 3, 1dc into next st, rep from * twice more, miss ch 3, 2tr into base of ch 3 at beg of round, sl st into top of ch3 at beg of round.

Round 5: Ch1, 1dc into 1st st, * ch3, 5trtog over next 5 sts, ch3 **, 1dc into next st, rep from * 3 more times, ending last rep at **, sl st into ch1 at beg of row.

Round 6: Ch1, 1dc into 1st st, * miss ch3, 5tr into centre of 5trtog, miss 3ch **, 1dc into next st, rep from * 3 more times, ending last rep at **, sl st into ch1 at beg of round.

Repeat rounds 3 – 6 once more, then rounds 3 – 5 again.

Fasten off yarn.

FINISHING

Weave in loose ends, block and press gently.

Make matching button loop as follows: Using G/6 hook, insert hook into centre stitch of back panel of case and work ch16, sl st into same chain to close loop.

Sew in loose ends, sew button to centre of front panel matching up with button loop.

MATERIALS

Rowan Creative Focus Worsted (75% wool, 25% alpaca; approx. 200m/ 220yd per 100g/3½oz ball), shade 1321 Delft x 1 ball 1.25cm (½in) button x 1

EQUIPMENT

Crochet hook 4mm (US size G/6)

GAUGE

Approx. 18 sts x 20 rows = 10cm (4in) in double crochet

FINISHED SIZE

Approx. 8cm x 12.5cm (3in x 5in)

EXPERIENCED

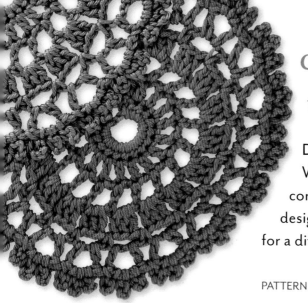

crochet cushion trim

Dress up a cushion with this lacy trim idea. Work through the main motif in the round, then complete the trim with partial sections of the main design. Use contrast colours or all the same shade for a different look.

MATERIALS
Patons Cotton DK (100% cotton; approx. 210m/ 230yd per 100g/3½oz ball)

A shade 2742 Fuchsia x 1 ball

Rowan Cotton Glacé (100% cotton; approx. 115m/125yd per 50g/1¾oz ball)

B shade 739 Dijon x 1 ball

C shade 724 Bubbles x 1 ball

Ready-made cushion

EQUIPMENT
Crochet hook size 3mm (US D/3)

GAUGE
Not crucial

FINISHED SIZE
Approx. 14cm (5½in)

PATTERN

full-size motif

Using 3mm (US D/3) hook and yarn A, ch10, join ends together with sl st to form ring.

Round 1: Ch2 (counts as 1htr), work 19htr into ring, sl st into top of ch2 at beg of round. (20 sts)

Round 2: Ch4, (counts as 1tr and ch1), * 1tr into next st, ch1; rep from * to end, sl st into 3rd ch of ch4 at beg of round.

Round 3: Ch5 (counts as 1tr and ch2), * 1tr into next st, ch2, miss ch1sp, rep from * to end, sl st into 3rd ch of ch5 at beg of round.

Round 4: Sl st into 1st ch2sp, ch3 (counts as 1tr), 2tr into same ch2sp, * ch1, 3tr into next ch2sp, rep from * to last ch2sp, ch1, sl st into top of ch3 at beg of round.

Round 5: Ch3, miss 3 sts,* 1dc into next ch1sp, ch3, rep from * to last ch1sp, sl st into base of ch3 at beg of round.

Round 6: Sl st into 1st ch3sp, ch6 (counts as 1tr and ch3), work 1tr into same ch3sp, * miss next st, work (1tr, ch3, 1tr) into next ch3sp, rep from * to end, sl st into 3rd of ch6 at beg of round.

Round 7: Sl st into 1st ch3sp, ch1, 1tr, make picot (MP) as follows: ch3, sl st into top of tr just worked, (1tr, MP) twice more into same ch3sp, * (1tr, MP) 3 times into next ch3sp, rep from * to end.

Break yarn and fasten off.

half motif

Make 1 in yarn B and 1 in yarn C.

Using 3mm (US D/3) hook and yarn B, ch10, join ends together with sl st to form ring.

Row 1: Ch2, 14htr into ring, turn. (14 sts)

Row 2: Ch4 (counts as 1tr and ch1), * 1tr into next st, ch1; rep from * to end, turn. (13 ch1sp's)

Row 3: Ch5 (counts as 1tr and ch2), * 1tr into next st, ch2, miss ch1sp, rep from * to end, turn.

Row 4: Sl st into 1st ch2sp, ch3 (counts as 1tr), work 2tr into same ch2sp, * ch1, 3tr into next ch2sp, rep from * to end, turn.

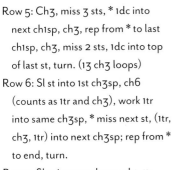

Row 5: Ch3, miss 3 sts, * 1dc into next ch1sp, ch3, rep from * to last ch1sp, ch3, miss 2 sts, 1dc into top of last st, turn. (13 ch3 loops)

Row 6: Sl st into 1st ch3sp, ch6 (counts as 1tr and ch3), work 1tr into same ch3sp, * miss next st, (1tr, ch3, 1tr) into next ch3sp; rep from * to end, turn.

Row 7: Sl st into 1st ch3sp, ch1, 1tr, make picot (MP) as follows: ch3, sl st into top of tr just worked, (1tr, MP) twice more into same ch3sp, * (1tr, MP) 3 times into next ch3sp, rep from * to end.

Break yarn and fasten off.

FINISHING

Weave in loose ends, then block and press to correct size.

Pin onto cushion and stitch into place.

earrings

These crocheted lace earrings will keep you trendy whatever the season. Crocheted using a fine thread and small hook, they look far more complicated than they actually are!

MATERIALS

Aunt Lydia's crochet thread Classic 10 (100% mercerized cotton; approx. 320m/ 350yd per 50g/1¾oz ball), 220812 Pumpkin x 1 ball

EQUIPMENT

Crochet hook size 2mm (US B/1)

Earring fish hooks x 2

GAUGE

Not crucial

FINISHED SIZE

Approx. 6.5cm x 4cm (2½in x 1½in)

SEE DIAGRAM PAGE 123

PATTERN (MAKE 2)

Using 2mm (US B/1) hook, ch6, join ends with sl st to form ring.

Round 1: Ch1, 12dc into ring, sl st into ch1 at beg of round.

Now work in rows to create lace pattern:

Row 1: Sl st into 1st 8 sts, ch5 (counts as 1tr and ch2), miss 1, (1tr, ch7, 1tr) into next st, ch2, miss 1, 1tr into next st, turn.

Row 2: Ch1, 1dc into 1st st, (1tr, ch1) 7 times into ch7sp, 1tr into same ch7sp, turn.

Row 3: Ch1, 1dc into 1st st, (1dc into next ch1sp, 1dc into next st) 3 times, ch4, miss ch1, (1dc into next ch1sp, 1dc into next st) 4 times, 1dc into last st, turn.

Row 4: Ch1, 1dc into 1st st, make picot (MP) as follows: ch3, sl st into dc just worked, (sl st into next 2 sts, 1tr into next, MP) twice, sl st into next st, work (2dc, 2htr, 1tr, MP, 2htr, 2dc) into ch4sp, sl st into next st, (1tr into next, MP, sl st into next 2 sts) twice, 1tr into last st, MP.

Fasten off yarn.

FINISHING

Weave in loose ends, gently block and press earring, pinning out picots.

Attach fish hooks to the centre top of earrings.

◄ projects

EXPERIENCED

covered buttons

The finishing touches are so important, and you can add that extra special detail with these crochet-covered buttons. The pattern will take you through how to crochet both round and square buttons as well as changing colour.

INTERMEDIATE

PATTERN

single colour 2cm (¾in) button

Using yarn A and 2mm (US B/1) hook, make a magic circle, insert hook into ring then draw through yarn, ch1.

Round 1: 8dc into magic circle then pull tight to close circle, sl st into ch1 at beg of round. (8 sts)

Round 2: Ch1, 2dc into each st, sl st into ch1 at beg of round. (16 sts)

Round 3: Ch1, 1dc into 1st st, * 2dc into next st, 1dc into next st, rep from * to last st, 2dc into last st, sl st into ch1 at beg of round. (24 sts)

Round 4: Ch1, 1dc into back loop of each st to end, join with sl st into ch1 at beg of round.

Round 5: Ch1, 1dc into 1st st, *2dctog over next 2 sts, 1dc into next st, rep from * to last 2 sts, 2dctog over last 2 sts, sl st into ch1 at beg of round. (16 sts)

Insert button.

Round 6: Ch1, 2dctog into 1st 2 sts, * 2dctog over next 2 sts, rep from * to end, sl st into ch1 at beg of round.

Fasten off yarn leaving a long enough tail to close up opening.

single colour 3.5cm (1¼in) button

Using yarn B and 2mm (US B/1) hook, work rounds 1–3 as given for 2cm (¾in) button.

Round 4: Ch1, 1dc into 1st 2 sts, * 2dc into next st, 1dc into next 2 sts, rep from * to last st, 2dc into last st, sl st into ch1 at beg of round. (32 sts)

Round 5: Ch1, 1dc into back loop of each st to end, join with sl st into ch1 at beg of round.

Round 6: Ch1, 1dc into 1st 2 sts, * 2dctog over next 2 sts, 1dc into next 2 sts, rep from * to last 2 sts, 2dctog over last 2 sts, sl st into ch1 at beg of round. (24 sts)

Round 7: Ch1, 1dc into 1st st, * 2dctog over next 2 sts, 1dc into next st, rep from * to last 2 sts, 2dctog over last 2 sts, sl st into ch1 at beg of round. (16 sts)

Insert button.

Round 8: Ch1, 2dctog into 1st 2 sts, * 2dctog over next 2 sts, rep from * to end, sl st into ch1 at beg of round.

Fasten off yarn leaving a long enough tail to close up opening.

MATERIALS

Anchor Artiste baby soft cotton No 5 (100% cotton; approx. 208m/227yd per 50g/1¾oz ball)

A shade Beige x 1 ball

Anchor Pearl Cotton, No 8 (100% cotton; approx. 85m/93yd per 10g/⅓oz ball)

B shade Bright blue x 1 ball

C shade Lilac x 1 ball

D shade Red x 1 ball

E shade Pale yellow x 1 ball

F shade Bright yellow x 1 ball

Round buttons, 1 each in following sizes: in 2cm (¾in), 3.5cm (1¼in), 4cm (1½in)

Square button, 1 x 1in (2.5cm)

EQUIPMENT

Crochet hook size 2mm (US B/1)

Sewing up needle

2 colour 4cm (1½in) button

Using yarn C and 2mm (US B/1) hook, work rounds 1 – 4 as given for single colour button but change to yarn D after round 3.

Round 5: Ch1, 1dc into 1st 3 sts, * 2dc into next st, 1dc into next 3 sts, rep from * to last st, 2dc into last st, sl st into ch1 at beg of round. (40 sts)

Round 6: Ch1, 1dc into back loop of each st to end, join with sl st into ch1 at beg of round.

Round 7: Ch1, 1dc into 1st 3 sts, * 2dctog over next 2 sts, 1dc into next 3 sts, rep from * to last 2 sts, 2dctog over last 2 sts, sl st into ch1 at beg of round.

Complete as given for single colour 3.5cm (1¼in) button.

2.5cm (1in) square button

Using yarn E and 2mm (US B/1) hook, make a magic circle, insert hook into ring then draw through yarn, ch1.

Round 1: 12dc into ring, sl st into ch1 at beg. (12 sts)

Round 2: Ch1, 1dc into 1st 2 sts, * 3dc into next st, 1dc into next 2 sts, rep from * until last st, 3dc into last st, sl st into ch1 at beg of round. (18 sts)

Fasten off yarn E and join in yarn F.

Round 3: Ch1, 1dc into 1st 3 sts, * 3dc into next st, 1dc into next 4 sts, rep from * twice more, 3dc into next st, 1dc into last st, sl st into ch1 at beg of round. (26 sts)

Round 4: ch1, 1dc into back loop of each st to end, join with sl st into ch1 at beg of round.

Round 5: Ch1, 1dc into 1st 3 sts, * 3dctog over next 3 sts, 1dc into next 4 sts, rep from * twice more, 3dctog over next 3 sts, 1dc into last st, sl st into ch1 at beg of round. (18 sts)

Insert button.

Round 6: Ch1, 1dc into 1st 2 sts, * 3dctog over next 3 sts, 1dc into next 2 sts, rep from * twice more, 3dctog over last 3 sts, sl st into ch1 at beg of round. (12 sts)

Fasten off yarn leaving a long enough tail to close up opening.

FINISHING

Weave in all loose ends.

zombie pin badge

Bring out your spooky side with these zombie badges. Worked in the round to create the head, with a few extra rows to define the jaw, they are the perfect base for adding embroidery and mismatched buttons.

PATTERN

Using your colour of choice and size 3mm (US D/3) hook, ch2.

Round 1: Work 8dc into 2nd ch from hook, sl st into ch1 at beg of round.

Round 2: Ch1, 2dc into each st to end. (16 sts)

Round 3: Ch1, 1dc into 1st st, * 2dc into next st, 1dc into next st, rep from * to last st, 2dc into last st, sl st into ch1 at beg of round. (24 sts)

Round 4: Ch1, 1dc into 1st 2 sts, * 2dc into next st, 1dc into next 2 sts, rep from * to last st, 2dc into last st, sl st into ch1 at beg of round. (32 sts)

Next Row: Ch2 (counts as 1htr), 1htr into next 7 sts, turn.

Next Row: Ch1, 2dctog over 1st 2 sts, 1dc into next 4 sts, 2dctog over last st and ch2.

Fasten off yarn.

FINISHING

Weave in loose ends, gently block and press into shape.

Using picture as a guide, sew buttons into position for eyes, then embroider mouth using black thread.

Sew brooch back onto the reverse side of badge.

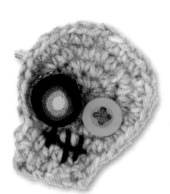

MATERIALS

Rowan Felted Tweed DK (50% merino wool, 25% alpaca, 25% viscose; approx. 175m/191yd per 50g/1¾oz ball)

A shade 159 Carbon x 1 ball

B shade 177 Clay x 1 ball

Rowan Fine Tweed (100% wool; approx. 90m/98yd per 25g/1oz ball)

C shade 381 Richmond x 1 ball

Brooch back, 1 per badge

Mixture of buttons, 2 per badge

Black embroidery thread

EQUIPMENT

Crochet hook size 3mm (US D/3)

GAUGE

Approx. 25 sts x 25 rows = 10cm (4in) in double crochet

FINISHED SIZE

Approx. 5.5cm (2in)

glasses chain

Fed up with misplacing your glasses? Then this is the project for you, created using a basic chain with the ends looped up for the arms of the glasses to sit in.

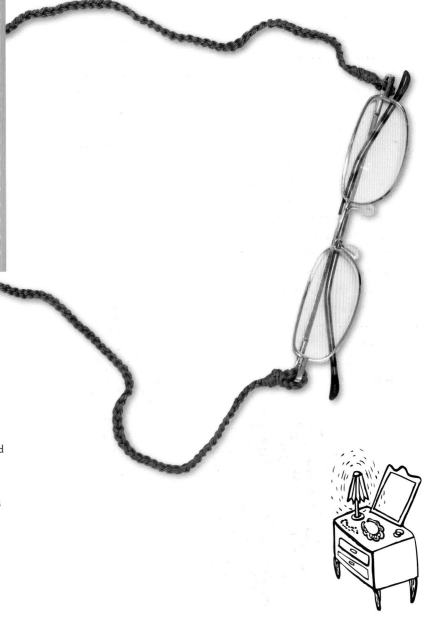

MATERIALS
Rowan Cotton Glacé (100% cotton; approx. 115m/125yd per 50g/1¾oz ball), shade 849 Windsor x 1 ball

EQUIPMENT
Crochet hook size 3mm (US D/3)

GAUGE
Approx. 27ch = 10cm (4in)

FINISHED SIZE
Approx. 60cm (23½in)

PATTERN

Using 3mm (US D/3) hook, ch9.
Row 1: Sl st into 1st ch to form loop, work a further 166ch, miss 8, sl st into the next ch.
Fasten off yarn.

FINISHING

Use the tails at the beginning and end of the chain to wrap around and cover the slip stitch.
Weave in loose ends and gently press chain with a steam iron.

bow tie

Call it geek or chic, this bow tie will make you stand out from the crowd. Worked in double crochet and embellished to create the plaid design, it couldn't be simpler!

PATTERN

Using yarn A and 4mm (US H/8) hook, ch12 +1 turning chain.

Row 1: 1dc into 2nd ch from hook, 1dc into each ch to end. (12 sts)

Row 2: Ch1, 1dc into each st to end, turn.

Repeat row 2 a further 24 times.

Break off yarn.

centre loop

Using yarn A and 4mm (US H/8) hook, ch3 +1 turning chain.

Row 1: 1dc into 2nd ch from hook, 1dc into each ch to end. (4 sts)

Row 2: ch1, 1dc into each st to end, turn.

Repeat row 2 a further 11 times.

Break off yarn.

FINISHING

Add plaid effect pattern by working a crochet chain into the fabric using the spaces and picture as a guide.

3 yarn B stripes lengthwise in 2nd, 6th and 10th spaces.

1 yarn E stripe lengthwise in 4th space.

2 yarn C stripes widthwise in 3rd and 23rd rows.

2 yarn D stripes in 5th and 21st rows.

FINISHING

Weave in loose ends, block and press gently.

ASSEMBLY

Fold main fabric in half with wrong sides together, then fold the outer edges in towards the centre crease. Pinch the centre and wrap the small length of fabric around the bow. Sew the short ends together to form a loop.

◄ projects

hair bow

This design is created in three separate sections. The large loops to each side are worked in a figure eight and layered up onto the bottom tie section. Everything is secured around the middle with a simple strip and a few stitches.

PATTERN

bow

Using 3.5mm (US E/4) hook, ch24, join with sl st to form a ring, then sl st into 12th ch to make a figure 8 shape.

Round 1: Ch1, 20dc into 1st loop, 20dc into 2nd loop, sl st into ch1 at beg of round.

Round 2: Ch1, sl st into 1st 2 sts, * 1dc into next 2 sts, 2htr into next st, 1htr into next st, 2tr into next st, 1tr into next st, 2dtr into next st, 1dtr into next 2 sts, 2dtr into next st, 1tr into next st, 2tr into next st, 1htr into next st, 2htr into next st, 1dc into next 2 sts **, sl st into next 4 sts, rep from * to ** once more, sl st into last 2 sts, sl st into ch1 at beg of round.

Break off yarn.

tails

Using 3.5mm (US E/4) hook, ch31.

Row 1: 1dtr into 4th ch from hook, 1dtr into next ch, 1tr into next 4ch, 1htr into next 4ch, 1dc into next 2ch, (2dctog over next 2ch) twice, 1dc into next 2 sts, 1htr into next 4ch, 1tr into next 4ch, 1dtr into last 2 sts.

Break off yarn.

middle section

Using 3.5mm (US E/4) hook, 30ch and fasten off.

ASSEMBLY

Block and press sections.

Place tails at the centre back of top bow, then wrap chain around middle section. Weave in ends to secure and finish.

MATERIALS
Brown Sheep Cotton Fleece (80% cotton, 20% merino wool; approx. 197m/215yd per 100g/3½oz ball), shade Caribbean Sea x 1 ball

EQUIPMENT
Crochet hook size 3.5mm (US E/4)

GAUGE
Not crucial

FINISHED SIZE
Approx. 6.5cm x 7cm (2½in x 2¾in)

SEE DIAGRAMS PAGE 122

flower headband

Whatever your hairstyle, this flower motif headband is a great accessory. The five-petal flower is worked in the round then stitched onto the extra long crochet chain tie.

MATERIALS

Rowan Revive (36% silk, 36% cotton, 28% viscose; approx. 125m/137yd per 50g/ 1¾oz ball), shade 473 Grit x 1 ball

EQUIPMENT

Crochet hook size 3mm (US D/3)

GAUGE

Not crucial

FINISHED SIZE

Approx. 8cm (3in)

PATTERN

flower

Using 3mm (US D/3) hook, ch6, join ends together with sl st to form ring.

Round 1: Ch1 (counts as 1dc), 15dc into ring, join with sl st into ch1 at beg of round.

Round 2: Ch9, sl st into 1st st, * ch2, miss2, sl st into next st, ch9, sl st into same place as last sl st, rep from * 3 more times, ch2, sl st into base of ch9 loop at beg of round.

Round 3: Sl st into 1st ch3 of ch9 loop, ch3 (counts as 1tr), work 3tr, ch2 4tr into same ch9 loop, * ch3, sl st into ch2sp, ch3,** work (4tr, ch2, 4tr) into next ch9 loop, rep from * ending last rep at **, sl st into top of ch3 at beg of round.

Fasten off yarn.

headband

Uisng 3mm (US D/3) hook, make a chain approx. 52 in (132 cm) long and fasten off.

ASSEMBLY

Sew flower motif approx. 38cm (15in) from the end of chain headband.

SEE DIAGRAM PAGE 125

bracelet

This project is a fun take on the classic chunky bracelet. Created by crocheting around a circular base made from strands of cotton, the fancy edge is then added to fan out from the base.

PATTERN

Using yarn A, make a circle approx. 7–8 cm (2¾–3 in) wide by wrapping the yarn 17 times around the top of a coffee mug or similar object. This will make the base of the bracelet that you will now cover with crochet.

Round 1: Insert hook into ring and using yarn B, draw yarn through and ch1, work 72dc into ring covering the base. If you need to add more stitches to cover the base add a multiple of 6. Join with sl st into ch1 at beg of round.

Round 2: Ch1, 1dc into 1st st, * miss 2, 7tr into next st, miss 2, 1dc into next st, rep from * ending last rep with sl st into ch1 at beg of round.
Break off yarn.

FINISHING

Weave in loose ends.

MATERIALS

Rowan Handknit Cotton (100% cotton; approx. 85m/93yd per 50g/1¾oz ball)

A shade 263 Bleached x 1 ball

Patons Cotton DK (100% cotton; approx. 210m/230yd per 100g/3½oz ball)

B shade 2724 Pomegranate x 1 ball

EQUIPMENT

Crochet hook size 3mm (US D/3)

GAUGE

Not crucial

FINISHED SIZE

Inside of bracelet, approx. 22cm (8¾in)

lace motif on purse

Be perfectly colour-coordinated with
this project idea. Make a simple
crochet motif using the yarn of your
choice then stitch into position
on the purse...a quick and
simple makeover.

MATERIALS

Rowan Cotton Glacé
(100% cotton; approx.
115m/125yd per
50g/1¾oz ball), shade
829 Twilight x 1 ball
Purse

EQUIPMENT

Crochet hook size
3mm (US D/3)

GAUGE

Not crucial

FINISHED SIZE

Approx. 8cm (3in) wide

SEE DIAGRAM PAGE 125

PATTERN

Using 3mm (US D/3) hook, ch8,
  join ends together with sl st to
  form ring.
Round 1: Ch3 (counts as 1tr), 2trtog
  into ring, * ch3, 3trtog into ring, rep
  from * 4 more times, ch3, sl st into
  top of ch3 at beg of round.
Round 2: Ch3 (counts as 1tr), 4tr
  into 1st ch3sp, * ch2, 5tr into next
  ch3sp, rep from * to end, ch2, sl st
  into ch3 at beg of round.
Round 3: Ch5, miss ch3 and 3tr, 1dc
  into next st,* ch3, miss ch3sp, 1dc
  into next st, ch5, miss 3 sts, 1dc into
  next st, rep from * 4 more times,

ch3, sl st into base of ch5 at
  beg of round.
Round 4: Sl st into 1st ch5sp, * (1tr,
  ch3, sl st into base of ch3 just
  worked to make picot) 5 times into
  ch5sp, sl st into next ch3sp, rep
  from * 5 more times.
Fasten off yarn.

FINISHING

Weave in loose ends and block and
  press to correct size.
Complete project by stitching motif
  onto a purse of your choice.

lace necklace

This delicate lace-effect necklace is worked in only a few rows and can easily be lengthened or shortened depending on the look you are going for. The design is finished off with a shell button and loop fastening that can be worn to the front as decoration.

PATTERN

Use 2.5mm (US C/2) hook.

Row 1: Ch5, * miss 3, 1tr into next ch 2, ch7, rep from * until 17 sets of 2tr's have been worked, turn.

Row 2: Sl st into each of the next 2tr and ch3sp, 3ch (counts as 1tr), (2trtog, ch3, 3trtog, ch3, 3trtog) into same ch3sp, * (3trtog, ch3) twice into next 3ch sp, 3trtog into same ch3sp, rep from * into each ch3sp to end.

ASSEMBLY

Weave in loose ends, block and press necklace, pinning out and stretching to peaked edge.

Make button loop by inserting hook into narrow edge of necklace, ch8. Fasten off yarn and sew open end of chain to make button loop. Sew button to opposite end.

MATERIALS

Rowan Siena 4 ply (100% cotton; approx. 140m/ 153yd per 50g/1¾oz ball), shade 652 Cream x 1 ball

Shell button x 1

EQUIPMENT

Crochet hook size 2.5mm (US C/2)

GAUGE

Approx. 5 repeats = 10cm (4in)

FINISHED SIZE

Approx. length 34cm (13½in)

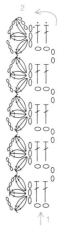

SEE DIAGRAM PAGE 124

peter pan collar

Dress your outfit up or down with this peter pan collar design. The collar is shaped slightly, allowing it to sit around the neck, with rounded peaks to the front and a button and loop fastening.

PATTERN

Using 5mm (US H/8) hook, ch70 + 1 turning ch.

Row 1: 1dc into each ch to end, turn. (70 sts)

Row 2: Ch1, 1dc into first 3 sts, * 2dc into next st, 1dc into next 6 sts, rep from * 8 more times, 2dc into next st, 1dc into last 3 sts, turn. (80 sts)

Rows 3 – 4: Ch1, 1dc into each st to end, turn.

Shape right-hand peak:

Next row: Ch1, 1dc into 20 sts, turn.

Next row: Ch1, miss 1, 1dc into each st to end, turn.

Next row: Ch1, 1dc into 15 sts, turn.

Next row: Ch1, miss 1, 1dc into each st to end, turn.

Next row: Ch1, 1dc into 10 sts, turn.

Next row: Ch1, miss 1, 1dc into each st to end, turn.

Next row: Ch1, 1dc into 5 sts, turn.

Next row: Ch1, miss 1, 1dc into each st to end, turn.

Work back across all the stitches to the left-hand side as follows:

Next row: Ch1, 1dc into 1st 4 sts, 1dc into missed st, * 1dc into next 4 sts, 1dc into missed st, rep from * twice, 1dc into each st to end, turn.

Shape left-hand peak the same as for right-hand peak.

Next row: Ch1, 1dc into 1st 4 sts, 1dc into missed st, *1dc into next 4 sts, 1dc into missed st, rep from * twice, 1dc into each st to end, turn.

Next row: Ch1, miss 2, 3tr into next st, 1htr into next st, 1dc into each st until 4 st rem, 1htr into next st, 3tr into next st, miss 2, sl st into ch1 at beg of prev row.

FINISHING

Weave in loose ends, block and press.

MATERIALS

Rowan Creative Focus Worsted (75% wool, 25% alpaca; approx. 219yds/ 200m per 3½oz/100g ball), shade 1890 Magenta x 1 ball

Button x 1

EQUIPMENT

Crochet hook 5mm (US H/8)

GAUGE

Approx. 16 sts x 21 rows = 4in (10cm) in double crochet

FINISHED SIZE

Approx. 17½ in (44cm) edge to edge, 2¾ in (7cm) deep at collar points

layered brooch

Show off your stitching skills with this layered lace brooch. The crochet motif is backed with a floral fabric puff and finished off with a tonal button and pretty ribbon.

MATERIALS

Anchor Aida 6 ply crochet thread count 10 (100% mercerized cotton; approx. 265m/290yd per 50g/1¾oz ball), shade 387 Beige x 1 ball

2 cm (¾in) button x 1

Cotton fabric, 15cm (6in) square

Ribbon, 10cm (4in) length

Brooch back

Sewing thread

EQUIPMENT

Crochet hook size 2mm (US B/1)

Sharp sewing needle

GAUGE

Not crucial

FINISHED SIZE

Approx. 5.5cm (2in) motif, 6.5cm (2½in) with fabric

PATTERN

With 2mm (US B/1) hook, ch6, join ends with sl st to form a ring.

Round 1: Ch1, 11dc into ring, sl st into ch1 at beg of round.

Round 2: Ch5 (counts as 1tr and ch2), * 1tr into next st, ch2, rep from * to end, sl st into 3rd of ch5 at beg of round. (12 ch2 spaces)

Round 3: Sl st into 1st ch2sp, ch3 (counts as 1tr), 2trtog, * ch3, 3trtog into next ch2sp, rep from * to end, ch3, sl st into top of ch3 at beg of round.

Round 4: Sl st into 1st ch3sp, ch1, * work [1dc, 1htr, 1tr, make picot (MP) as follows, 3ch, sl st into top of tr just worked, 1htr, 1dc] into same ch3sp, work (1dc, 1htr, MP, 1dc) into next ch3sp, rep from * to end.

Fasten off yarn.

fabric circle

Cut a 12.5cm (5in) circle from cotton fabric and work a running stitch approx. 0.5cm (¼in) in from the edge. Pull ends tight to close circle, then knot the ends to secure.

FINISHING

Weave in ends, block, and press.

ASSEMBLY

Using picture as a guide, layer everything up as follows:

Fold ribbon in half and place in centre of fabric circle with gathered opening facing up the way, then place the crochet motif on top, then place button at the centre of the crochet motif and sew through all the layers.

Sew brooch back to the underside of layered motif.

SEE DIAGRAM PAGE 125

scarf

This super chunky scarf is worked in one continual length. Each motif is crocheted from the centre out then linked together with slip stitches to hold everything in place.

PATTERN

first motif

Using 12mm (US P) hook, ch10, join ends together to form ring.

Row 1: Ch3 (counts as 1tr), work 9tr into ring, turn. (10 sts)

Row 2: Ch4 (counts as 1tr and ch1), * (1tr, ch1) into next st, rep from * 7 more times, 1tr into last st, turn. (9 ch1sp)

Row 3: * Ch3, miss ch1, sl st into next st, rep from * to end, turn.

second motif

Row 1: Ch6, sl st into top of tr from row 1 of first motif to form a ring.

Row 2: Ch3 (counts as 1tr), sl st into centre ring from 1st motif, work 9tr into ch6 ring, turn.

Row 3: Ch4 (counts as 1tr and ch1), * (1tr, ch1) into next st, rep from * 7 more times, 1tr into last st, turn. (9 ch1sp)

Row 4: * Ch3, miss ch1, sl st into next st; rep from * to end.

third motif

Turn work so the rounded edge from first motif is to the top.

Row 1: Ch6, sl st into top of tr from row 1 of last motif to form a ring.

Row 2: Ch3 (counts as 1tr), work 9tr into ch6 ring, turn.

Row 3: Ch4 (counts as 1tr and ch1), * (1tr, ch1) into next st, rep from * 7 more times, 1tr into last st. (9 chsp)

Row 4: Sl st into 2nd ch3 loop of motif to the LHS, turn, ch3, sl st into 1st st, * ch3, miss ch1, sl st into next st, rep from * to end.

Repeat last motif until 10 motifs in total have been worked or required length, turning the work to make sure that the rounded edge of the motif to the left is at the top.

Break yarn and fasten off.

FINISHING

Weave in loose ends, then pin out scarf, and block to dimensions. Link motifs with slip stitches.

MATERIALS

Rowan Drift (100% merino wool; approx. 80m/87yd per 100g/3½oz ball), shade 905 Plantation x 1

EQUIPMENT

Crochet hook size 12mm (US P)

GAUGE

Approx. 12.5cm x 18cm (5in x 7in) per motif

FINISHED SIZE

Approx. 25cm x 120cm (10in x 47in)

SEE DIAGRAM PAGE 124

EXPERIENCED

cloche hat

This is the perfect pull-on hat. The cloche design means it sits snug around the ears and looks cute at a jaunty angle. It's a good way to practise working in the round, and the more experienced crocheter will easily complete it within 30 minutes.

PATTERN

Using 9mm (US M/13) hook, make a magic circle.

Round 1: 7htr into loop then pull tight to close, work sl st into top of 1st st.

Round 2: Ch2, 2htr into each st to end, join with sl st into ch1 at beg of round. (16 sts)

Round 3: Ch2, 1htr into 1st st,* 2htr into next st, 1htr into next st, rep from * to last st, 2htr into last st, join with sl st into ch1 at beg of round. (24 sts)

Round 4: Ch2, 1htr into each st to end, join with sl st into ch1.

Round 5: Ch2, 1htr into 1st 2 sts, * 2htr into next st, 1htr into next 2 sts, rep from * to last st, 2htr into last st. (32 sts)

Round 6: As round 4.

Round 7: Ch2, 1htr into 1st 3 sts, * 2htr into next st, 1htr into next 3 sts, rep from * to last st, 2htr into last st. (40 sts)

Rounds 8 – 14: As round 4.

shape brim

Round 15: Ch2, 1htr into next 7 sts, 1bptr into next 24 sts, 1htr into each st to end, join with sl st into ch2 at beg of round.

Round 16: Ch2, 1htr into next 8 sts, 1tr into next 25 sts, 1htr into each st to end, join with sl st into ch2 at beg of round.

Round 17: As round 4.

Fasten off yarn.

FINISHING

Weave in loose ends and gently block.

MATERIALS

Rowan Big Wool (100% merino wool; approx. 80m/87½yd per 100g/3½oz ball), shade 43 Forest x 1 ball

EQUIPMENT

Crochet hook size 9mm (US M/13)

GAUGE

Approx. 9 sts x 6 rows = 10cm (4in) in half double crochet

TO FIT

Average adult

EXPERIENCED

belt

Up-cycle an existing belt with this project idea. The belt strap is made of simple crochet chains plaited together and can be worked to fit any length. The belt can be narrow or wide depending on the type of buckle.

PATTERN

Using 5mm (US H/8) hook, ch130 or work chain until strip measures approx. 76cm (30in).

Break off yarn.

Make 11 more chains to match the first.

ASSEMBLY

Take 6 chains and place flat with the tops all matching up, then safety pin through all 6 to hold the tops together.

Divide the chains into 3 pairs and braid together. When you reach the end, safety pin them together to stop the braid from unravelling.

Repeat with the remaining chains.

Secure the top section by working a line of back stitch across all 6 chains using a sharp sewing needle and matching thread. Repeat this process so both sections have been secured along the top.

Lay both sections side by side, then mark where you want the end of the belt to be – remember to take into consideration the type of belt buckle or strap you have.

Once you are happy with the length, work a line of back stitch across first section and repeat with second section.

Decide which side you want to be the right side, and sew the strips together using sewing up needle and yarn.

Weave in loose ends and attach each end to belt buckle and strap.

MATERIALS

Rowan Summer Tweed (70% silk, 30% cotton; approx. 120m/131yd per 50g/1¾oz ball), shade 530 Toast x 1 ball

1 x recycled belt buckle and strap approx 4cm (1½in) wide

EQUIPMENT

Crochet hook size 5mm (US H/8)

4 x medium safety pins

Sharp sewing needle and thread to match

Sewing up needle

GAUGE

Not crucial

FINISHED SIZE

Approx. 76cm (30in)

ring

The ring shank is made from yarn and wire worked together throughout and can easily be changed to fit any size finger. The beaded embellishments bring a touch of sparkle to the occasion, so go to town!

PATTERN

Using yarn A and B held together, ch4 + 1 turning ch.

Row 1: 1sc into 2nd ch from hook, 1dc into each ch to end, turn. (4 sts)

Row 2: Ch1, 1dc into each st to end.

Repeat last row another 11 times.

Fasten off yarn, leaving long enough length to sew ends together.

FINISHING

Sew ends together to make a ring, and weave in loose ends.

Create the centre flat section of the ring by folding over the first 4 and last 4 rows, then roll between finger and thumb to round off.

Add decoration to the centre section as follows: Using an embroidery needle and turquoise thread, weave in and out of the stitches to fill in the gaps.

Using the picture as a guide, add the beaded decoration as follows: Thread sharp sewing needle with yellow yarn, bring needle up through the turquoise section where you want the bead to sit, thread oval bead and seed bead onto the needle and slip down onto the surface of the ring. Next, bring the needle back down the oval bead and out towards the back of the ring. Repeat this process with all the beads, working 3 on the first line, then 2 on the next line, then 3 and 2 on the following lines.

MATERIALS

Anchor Pearl No 8 (100% cotton; approx. 85m/93yd per 10g/ $^1/_3$oz ball)

A shade Bright Yellow x 1 ball

Scientific Wire Company coloured craft wire 0.2mm (approx. 175m/191yd per reel)

B shade 3006 Light Gold x 1 reel

10 x yellow seed beads

10 x Guterman 0.5cm (¼in) flat oval beads, ref. 603007

Small amount of turquoise blue embroidery thread

EQUIPMENT

Crochet hook size 3mm (US D/3)

Embroidery needle

Sharp sewing needle

GAUGE

Not crucial

FINISHED SIZE

Approx. 2cm (¾in) wide

equipment

essential kit

Once you have chosen to embark on a crochet odyssey, you'll need a few things to get you on your way. A local yarn store will almost certainly be able to get you started with some equipment for crocheting, but don't underestimate the shopping potential of the internet. There are hundreds, possibly thousands, of online craft stores that carry all the items you'll ever need. Build a good relationship with your local yarn store – it's great to support your community. They might even be able to suggest crochet social groups and outings, or even offer classes or workshops to improve your skills. You'll need the following items to get started:

CROCHET HOOKS

These come in various sizes, from 1mm for tiny and intricate lace work, up to large 15mm and even 25 or 30mm hooks for super chunky yarn. We recommend starting with a 4mm hook (US size D), for standard knitting yarn (called double knitting or 8 ply). If you want to start with a larger hook and thicker yarn, this might help you to see the stitches more clearly. You'll need a 5mm (US size H) hook for aran (worsted) weight yarn, or an 6.5mm (US size L) hook for chunky (bulky) yarn.

YARN
(see pages 100–101).

OTHER ITEMS

These include scissors for cutting yarn, a large blunt darning needle for sewing in ends, stitch markers, embroidery threads and sharp sewing needles.

Any other haberdashery items or embellishments in your sewing box can be used to adorn your work. These can include buttons, beads and sequins.

a note about yarn

Once you have decided to learn to crochet, the fun part is choosing your yarn. Don't be restricted by what the pattern says; if you have seen some sumptuous yarn on sale, then go for it! All the patterns in this book have suggested yarn to use and that is the yarn used for the example block. However, you need not be restricted to that yarn at all – you can substitute almost any yarn as long as you use the right size hook. If you're making a granny square and you want it thick and chunky, use a chunky weight yarn or wool. Or if you want tiny, delicate ones then use a 4 ply or lace weight yarn instead. You don't need to use crochet cotton for your crochet, you can use any material. Even torn-up old T-shirts can be given a new lease on life with giant crochet hooks! To help you, here is a basic chart so you have the right tools for the job. Check the band on the yarn first for needle and hook size suggestions, but if you're not sure, then check below.

hooks and yarns

yarn weight	hook size (metric)	(letter)
4 ply (fingering or sock yarn)	2.5mm/3mm	B
double knitting/8 ply (also known as DK)	3.5mm/4mm	E/G
aran (worsted)	5mm/5.5mm	H/I/J
chunky (also known as bulky)	6mm/6.5mm	J/L
super chunky (also known as super bulky)	7mm – 20mm	N/P

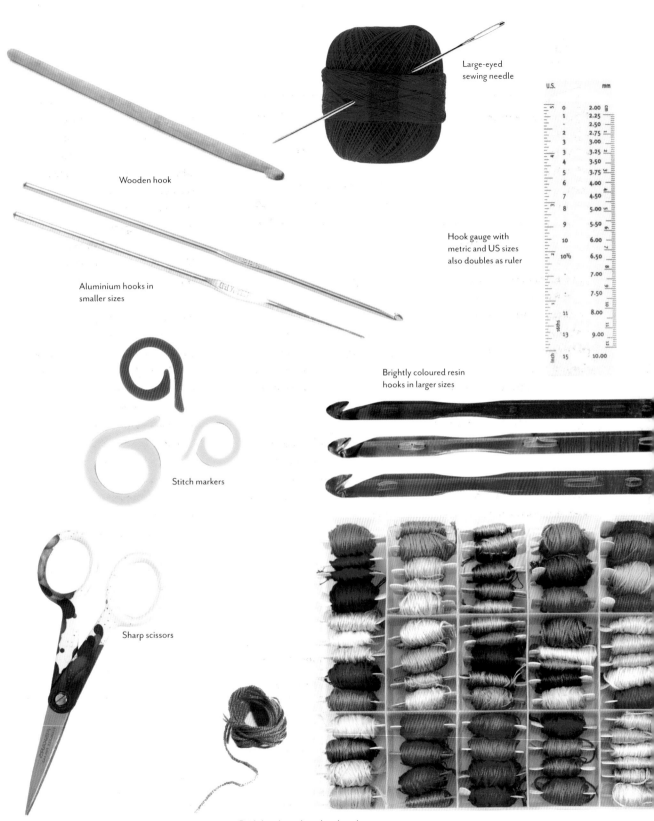

Wooden hook

Large-eyed
sewing needle

Aluminium hooks in
smaller sizes

Hook gauge with
metric and US sizes
also doubles as ruler

U.S.		mm
	0	2.00
	1	2.25
	.	2.50
	2	2.75
	3	3.00
	3	3.25
	4	3.50
	5	3.75
	6	4.00
	7	4.50
	8	5.00
	9	5.50
	10	6.00
	10½	6.50
		7.00
		7.50
	11	8.00
	13	9.00
	15	10.00

Brightly coloured resin
hooks in larger sizes

Stitch markers

Sharp scissors

Brightly coloured crochet threads

yarn weights

Yarn 'weight' refers to the thickness of the yarn. Names for
the different weights vary from country to country, as do the
yarns within each category. The gauge and recommended
hook sizes are guidelines only. You'll want to match the
gauge of the pattern you are crocheting, but knowing the
weight of a yarn is important should you decide to substitute
one yarn for another.

laceweight/2 or 3 ply
The gauge for these yarns varies and so does the fibre content.
Crochet threads are in this weight category.

superfine/fingering weight/sock/4 ply
These yarns are most often used for baby and children's clothing and, of course, socks. Gauge
is 21–32 stitches to 10cm (4in) with recommended hook sizes 2.25–3.5mm (B/1 to E/4).

fine/sportweight/baby
These yarns are also a good choice for baby items and socks. Gauge is 16–20 stitches to 10cm
(4in) with recommended hook sizes 3.5–4.5mm (E/4 to 7).

8 ply/double knitting (DK)/light worsted

Double knitting weight is also referred to as a 'light' worsted weight and is suitable for many projects. Gauge is 12–17 stitches to 10cm (4in) with recommended hook sizes 4–4.5mm (7 to I/9).

medium/fisherman/aran/worsted weight/12 ply

A versatile and common weight of yarn that is a good choice for many crochet projects. Gauge is 11–14 stitches to 10cm (4in) with recommended hook sizes 5–6mm (I/9 to K/10½).

bulky/chunky

Bulky yarns are typically used for outerwear and rugs. Gauge is 9–11 stitches to 10cm (4in) with recommended hook sizes 6.5–9mm (K/10½ to M and N/13).

super bulky

Super bulky is a craft weight yarn that works up quickly on the largest sizes of crochet hooks. Gauge is 5–9 stitches to 10cm (4in) with recommended hook sizes 9mm (M and N/13) and larger.

reading a pattern

The patterns in this book are written in abbreviations, all of which can be found in the chart below. Follow the instructions in the pattern, using this guide to work out the stitches used in the pattern.

full stitch name	abbreviation
begin (s)/beginning	beg
back loop	bl
chains(s)	ch(s)
centimetres	cm
double crochet	dc
decrease	dec
double treble crochet	dtr
front loop	fl
half treble crochet	htr
inch (es)	in(s)
increase	inc
pattern	patt
previous	prev
remaining	rem
repeat	rep
right side of crocheted fabric	rs
single crochet (US only)	sc
slip stitch	sl st
space	sp

full stitch name	abbreviation
stitches (es)	st(s)
wrong side	ws
together	tog
treble crochet	tr
wrong side of crocheted fabric	ws

Note: Stitch patterns include instructions for creating multiple repeats so you can make the correct number of stitches necessary for your first row, and they allow you to make fabrics as large as you wish. For example, to create two pattern repeats of a pattern multiple of 4 + 1 (add 1 to beg ch), you would calculate 4 x 2 equals 8, add 1 to equal 9, and then add 1 more to your chain to equal 10. For a three-pattern repeat, you would need to make 14 chain stitches and so on.

PUNCTUATION

Patterns use abbreviations and contain other punctuation marks to produce a concise and easy-to-read set of instructions. They also help avoid needless repetition. Once you understand the mechanics, reading patterns will become second nature to you.

( ) Round brackets give you additional information about the pattern. For example (12 tr) listed at the end of a row indicates that you should have twelve treble crochet stitches when a row has been completed. Ch 3 (counts as a tr) indicates that your chain 3 turning chain counts as a treble crochet stitch, and the stitch is included in the instructions for the stitch count at the end of the row or round.

* An asterisk is used to indicate stitch instructions and pattern repeats on a row or round. * Dc, ch 1, miss next. Rep from * 4 times to last, dc in last. This instruction tells you to double crochet, chain 1, miss the next stitch. You will repeat the direction four more times and when you arrive at the last stitch, you will double crochet into it.

CROCHET

US	UK
chain (ch)	chain (ch)
single crochet (sc)	double crochet (dc)
half double crochet (hdc)	half treble (htr)
double crochet (dc)	treble (tr)
treble (tr)	double treble (dtr)
double treble (dtr)	quadruple treble (quad tr)
slip stitch (ss)	slip stitch (sl st)
together (tog)	together (tog)
yarn over hook (yoh)	yarn round hook (yrh)
skip (sk)	miss (miss)
wrong side (ws)	wrong side (ws)
right side (rs)	right side (rs)

how to crochet

Take some time over these instructions, and remember that practice makes perfect. These can easily work whether you are left- or right-handed – use the hook in the hand that you write with. You can hold it like a pencil, or with the hook underneath your hand (the 'knife hold'). Hold the hook however feels comfortable – there is no 'right' or 'wrong' way.

slip knot

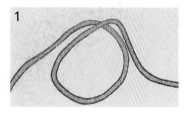
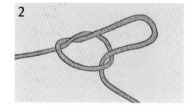
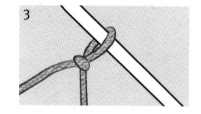

To begin almost all crochet, you'll need to make a slip knot. You will need to have a longish bit of yarn ready. Make a loop with the yarn and pull the tail end (the end not attached to the ball of yarn) through and tighten. Pop that slip knot onto the crochet hook and tug sharply to pull it tight.

holding the yarn

Once the slip knot is on the hook, hold your left hand out, palm up, or vice versa if you are left-handed.

Slot the tail of the yarn between your pinkie and ring fingers and wrap it around the back of your hand. Point your index finger out and rest the yarn on your finger.

Another method of holding the working yarn is to place it over your first finger, then bring your fingers in towards your palm, holding onto the yarn lightly.

making a chain

The foundation chain is the beginning of almost all the blocks in this book. Once done, it resembles a braid or a series of 'V' shapes.

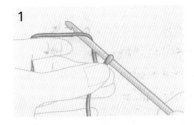
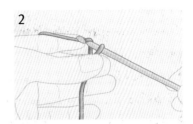

Bring the hook under the yarn that rests on your index finger. Clasp the yarn around the hook and pull it through the loop on the hook. Repeat this until you have the desired amount of stitches. Count each chain stitch as you work them, but do not count the loop on your hook.

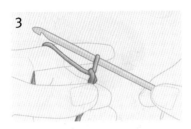

how to slip stitch

This stitch is used for joining, or working along to the next point in the pattern while being invisible. As you did for the foundation chain, insert the hook through the chain and wrap the yarn round hook (YRH) by bringing your hook under the yarn resting on your finger and drawing it through the loop. You'll now have 2 loops on your hook. Draw the first one through the second one, leaving you with 1 loop on the hook.

turning chain

You will need to work some extra chains at the end of each row or round for turning – how many chains will depend on what stitch you are doing. The turning chain ensures there are enough stitches in the row overall, so add the following number of extra chains on your foundation to make sure you have enough stitches in the row:

For double crochet, 1 chain
For treble crochet, 3 chains
For double treble crochet, 4 chains
For quadruple treble, 5 chains

You will also work a turning chain at the beginning of each row. This will sometimes count as the first stitch of your round or row. Some crocheters find it simple to work the turning chain BEFORE turning their work, but only do this when working back and forth along the foundation chain.

working in rounds

There are three methods of beginning a round, and your pattern will have instructions for which method to use, but feel free to use a different method if none is suggested by the pattern.

MAKING A JOINED ROUND OF CHAINS

This is a good way to begin if your first round has a large number of stitches, but you will have a hole in the centre of your fabric. It will allow the stitches of the first round to lie flat, without bunching or overlapping. You can also add additional chains to accommodate more stitches in the beginning round.

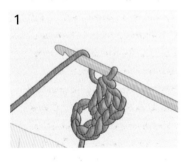

Begin by making a short chain. Join the chain into a ring by making a slip stitch into the first chain. Work a turning chain (see page 105) to bring the round up to the proper height of your stitches, then work the first round of stitches into the ring. To join the first round together, work a slip stitch into the top chain of the turning chain.

CREATING A ROUND OF STITCHES BY WORKING INTO ONE CHAIN

This method is easy to work and will give you a tight centre without a hole, but it is not a good choice if you have a large number of stitches in the first round as too many stitches will cause the first round to be overcrowded and it will not lie flat.

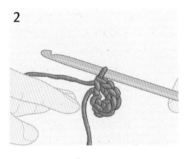

For example, chain 2, and work 6 double crochet stitches into the second chain from your hook. Work under the top loop only of the chain stitch. If you work only under the top loop, you will find that you will be able to expand and tighten the chain as needed.

YARN MAGIC RING

This is the method of choice for a really tight centre round that has a lot of stitches. However, do not use this method when working with slippery yarns because the yarn end may work loose.

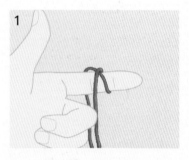

Encircle the yarn around your forefinger anticlockwise and cross it over the working yarn. Make sure to leave at least a 15cm (6in) tail for weaving in later.

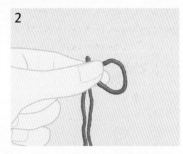

Slide the loop off your finger while pinching the 'x' overlap you just made.

3

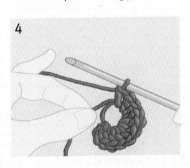

Insert your hook in front of the loop but behind your working yarn.

4

Pull up a loop with the working yarn and hold it on your hook with your forefinger. Yarn over and ch1 to secure. Crochet over both the loop and yarn tail as you complete the first round. Pull the yarn tail to tighten.

WORKING TUBULAR ROUNDS

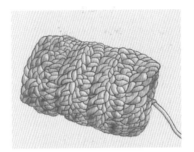

Begin with a length of chain stitches equal to the diameter you wish your tube to be. Slip stitch into the first chain to join the round. Work a turning chain to bring the round up to height. Work 1 stitch into each chain, being careful not to twist the chain as you work, and join the round at the end. To achieve a straight seam, turn your work at the end of each round; otherwise, you will have a slanted seam.

Evenly work (1 stitch in each stitch) in the following rounds.

To create a tube with a closed end, work flat rounds to the diameter required for your tube to make the closed end, then work evenly until your tube is the desired height.

WORKING FLAT ROUNDS

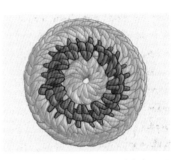

Complete a round of stitches and slip stitch into the first stitch to join the round. Begin the next round with a turning chain to bring the round to the correct height, but do not turn your work (unless instructed to do so in your pattern). The turning chain doesn't always count as a stitch; check with the pattern you are working. Work 2 stitches into each stitch of the previous round for round 2.

For round 3 and the following rounds, you will increase your stitch count by the same number of stitches that you made in round 1.

The granny square table runner project (page 46) is a motif example of working flat rounds.

double crochet

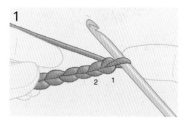

1

This small stitch is tight and neat, perfect for working with shapes. After you have made the foundation chain, count the stitches back from the hook. Insert the hook into the second 'V' along the hook.

2

Wrap the yarn around the hook and draw it back through this stitch. You will now have 2 loops on the hook.

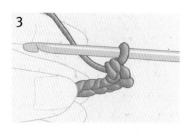

3

Wrap the YRH again and draw it through both loops on the hook. You have made a double crochet! Continue into every stitch until you get to the end of the foundation row.

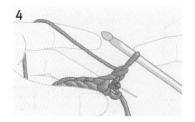

4

To work the next row, chain 1 and turn your work. Insert your hook into the first stitch under the top 2 loops and complete steps 2 and 3. Continue working double crochet stitches across the row. You do not work a stitch into the turning chain of the previous row.

half treble crochet

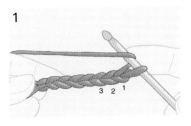

1

Yarn over and insert your hook into the third chain from your hook.

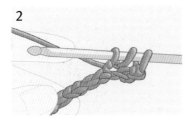

2

Yarn over and pull up a loop. You will have 3 loops on your hook.

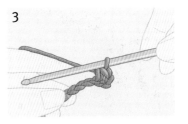

3

Yarn over and draw through all 3 loops on your hook to complete the stitch. Yarn over, insert your hook into the next chain, and complete steps 2 and 3. Repeat into each chain across.

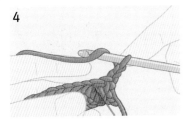

4

To work the next row, chain 2 and turn your work. Insert your hook into the second stitch (missing the first stitch because the chain 2 counts as a stitch). Do not work into turning chain unless pattern requires.

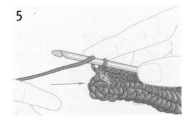

5

Work under the top 2 loops and complete steps 2 and 3. Continue working stitches into each stitch across the row. Your last stitch was made into the top chain of the previous row's turning chain.

Note: Be aware that some patterns using this stitch do not count the chain 2 turning chains as a stitch, because it tends to leave gaps in the row edges. If that happens, you would work the first stitch of your row into the first stitch, and you would not work a stitch into the turning chain at the end of the row. Follow the pattern instructions closely and make sure your stitch count for each row or round matches the stitch count given in the pattern.

treble crochet

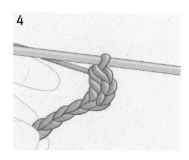

Yarn round and insert your hook into the fourth chain from your hook.

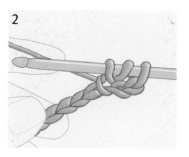

Yarn round and pull up a loop. You will have 3 loops on your hook.

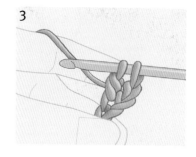

Yarn round and draw through 2 loops. You will have 2 loops on your hook.

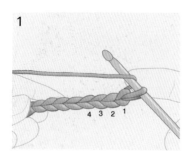

Yarn round and draw through 2 loops to complete the stitch. Yarn round, insert your hook into the next chain, and complete steps 2 to 4. Repeat into each chain across.

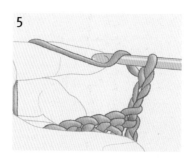

To work the next row, chain 3 and turn your work. Insert your hook into the second stitch (skipping the first stitch because the chain 3 counts as a stitch). Work under the top 2 loops and complete steps 2 to 4.

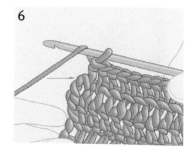

Continue working stitches into each stitch across the row. Your last stitch will be made into the top chain of the previous row's turning chain.

double treble crochet

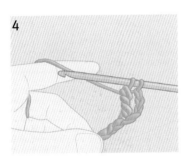

1

Yarn round twice and insert your hook into the fifth chain from your hook.

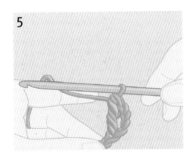

2

Yarn round and pull up a loop. You will have 4 loops on your hook.

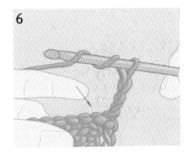

3

Yarn round and draw through 2 loops. You will have 3 loops on your hook.

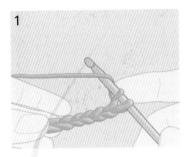

4

Yarn round and draw through 2 loops. You will have 2 loops on your hook.

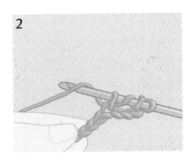

5

Yarn round and draw through 2 loops to complete the stitch. Yarn over twice and insert your hook into the next chain and complete steps 2 to 4. Repeat into each chain across.

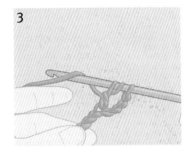

6

To work the next row, chain 4 and turn your work. Insert hook into the second stitch (missing the first stitch because the chain 4 counts as a stitch). Work under the top 2 loops and complete steps 2 to 5. Continue working stitches into each stitch across the row. Your last stitch will be made into the top chain of the previous row's turning chain.

symbol crochet charts

Symbol crochet charts are a 'picture' of the crocheted piece and may be a complete chart or a section that represents multiple stitch repeats. Each stitch needed to create the piece is represented by a symbol on the chart so written instructions are not necessary.

Crochet patterns will often include chart or graph instructions along with the written ones. Charts use symbols to represent each stitch and can show you at a glance what you are going to be doing and where you are in a pattern. They are a very useful visual representation of how the fabric is constructed. Charts are read slightly differently, depending on whether the pattern is worked in rows or in the round.

ROW-BY-ROW CHARTS

Row-by-row charts, which are read from the bottom up, start by showing you the foundation chain; this is the starting point, as with written instructions. When working in rows crochet is usually turned at the end of each row, this does not change when working from a chart unless stated.

• Right-side rows are worked from right to left; wrong-side rows go from left to right

• A row number shows where the row begins and an arrow shows from what direction you are reading the chart

• You alternate from right side to wrong side with each row

CHARTS IN THE ROUND

When working a crochet fabric in the round you start from the centre and work your way outwards always going in an anticlockwise direction and with the right side of the fabric facing. This is exactly the same when reading from this type of chart. You start by creating a centre ring then begin the pattern as shown by working into this ring completing the round by joining them together with a slip stitch.

• Read the circular charts anticlockwise

• A number will show where the round begins and an arrow will show from what direction you are reading the chart

• You don't need to turn the work at the end of the round – the right side of the fabric is always facing you

• It is important to mark the beginning of the round, especially when working smaller stitches such as the double crochet; it's a good idea to place a marker at the beginning of the round

+	double crochet (sc)
◯	chain (ch)
⬤	slip stitch (sl st)
T	half treble crochet (htr)
⊤ (treble)	treble crochet (tr)
⊤ (double treble)	double treble crochet (dtr)
♧	picot
A	treble crochet 2 tog (tr24og)
A	treble crochet 3 tog (tr3tog)
shell	5 treble crochet shell

measuring gauge

What exactly is gauge? Gauge (or 'tension') is all about ensuring that your finished crocheted piece is the exact size you or the pattern intended. If two crocheters make a double crochet swatch using the same yarn and crochet hook, chances are the swatches will be different sizes. If you don't take the time to check your gauge, you may have disastrous results, especially if you are making a garment.

Each pattern will indicate the gauge. For example: 10cm (4in) = 15 treble crochet (tr) and 9 rows using 5mm (H) hook.

To check your gauge, crochet a 15cm (6in) swatch using the hook size, yarn and stitch pattern (in this example, treble crochet) called for in the instructions. Place a ruler horizontally across a stitch row in the centre of the swatch and insert pins at the zero and 10cm (4in) mark. Count the stitches between your pins. Do you have fourteen treble crochets? If you have too many stitches, use a larger hook. If you have too few, use a smaller hook. Check the row height by taking a vertical measurement in the same way. Continue making swatches until you achieve the correct gauge with whatever size hook you need to achieve the results.

It is also a good idea to recheck the gauge often while crocheting your project. Your gauge may vary from one sitting to the next and can change when you relax or when you get stressed.

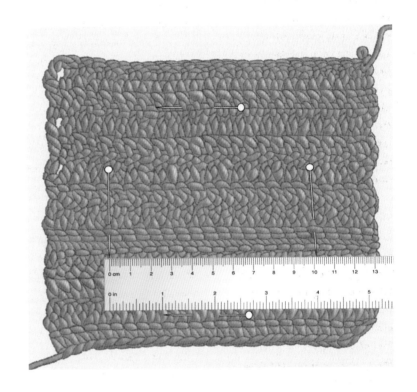

increasing and decreasing shaping

Achieving basic shaping skills is easy once you have learned the basics of increasing and decreasing your stitches. These techniques are essential for many crochet projects. Decrease stitches are worked over two (or more) stitches and combine several stitches in one stitch. The steps illustrate a one-stitch decrease for the four basic crochet stitches.

TO INCREASE THE NUMBER OF STITCHES WITHIN A ROW OR ROUND

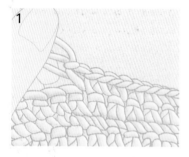

You simply place more than 1 stitch into a stitch of the previous row or round. Here increasing is shown in double crochet, but you increase the same way for all the other stitches.

TO INCREASE BY SEVERAL STITCHES AT THE BEGINNING OF A ROW

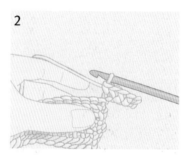

Make the required number of turning chains and then add a chain for each additional stitch you want to add. Miss the turning chains and work a stitch into the remaining chains to complete your increase.

Note: If you are working a flat piece of crochet and need to increase a few stitches but the pattern doesn't specify exactly where, it's best to work the increase at least one stitch in from the edge, as this will make your work neater.

DOUBLE CROCHET DECREASE

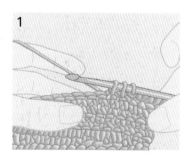

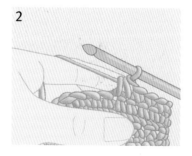

Insert the hook into the first stitch and pull up a loop. Insert the hook into the next stitch and pull up a loop. You will have 3 loops on your hook. Yarn round and draw through all 3 loops.

HALF TREBLE CROCHET DECREASE

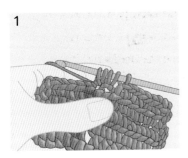

1

Yarn round, insert the hook into the first stitch, and pull up a loop. Yarn over*, insert hook in the next stitch, and pull up a loop. You will have 5 loops on your hook.

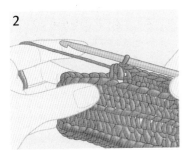

2

Yarn round and draw through all 5 loops.

* For a less bulky half treble crochet decrease, omit this yarn round.

TREBLE CROCHET DECREASE

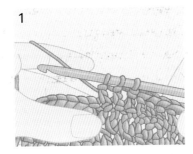

1

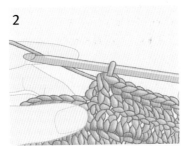

2

Yarn round, insert the hook into the first stitch, and pull up a loop. Yarn round and draw through 2 loops on hook. Yarn round, insert hook into the next stitch, and pull up a loop. Yarn round and draw through 2 loops. You will have 3 loops on your hook. Yarn over and draw through all 3 loops.

DOUBLE TREBLE CROCHET DECREASE

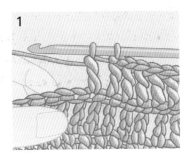

1

This decrease is worked similarly to the treble crochet decrease. Work a double treble crochet into the first stitch until you have 2 loops on your hook, omitting the last step.

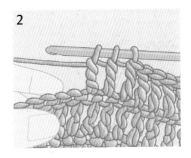

2

Yarn round twice, insert your hook into the next stitch and work double treble crochet until 3 loops remain on your hook.

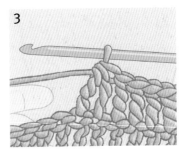

3

Yarn over and draw through all 3 loops to complete the decrease.

joining in a new yarn or colour

Often, you'll want to change to a new ball of yarn or yarn colour at the end of a row, but you may also need to do it within a row, when indicated in the pattern. The technique for doing both is the same.

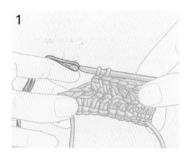

Work the last stitch but stop at the last step before drawing through the final yarn round. You will have 2 loops on your hook.

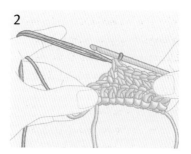

Drop the old yarn/colour behind your work and draw the new yarn/colour through to complete the stitch. Continue working with the new yarn/colour as usual.

Note: Unless the pattern specifies, it's best to change colour at the beginning of a row rather than in the middle.

You can work over the ends of the old and new yarn to avoid having to weave or sew them in later. This will save time but it can make the fabric slightly bulkier.

weaving in ends

After completing a piece of fabric, and before blocking and pressing, you need to weave in all your loose ends. It is best to use a tapestry needle with a large eye and blunt tip.

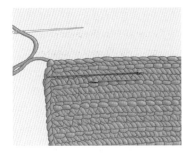

Weave in the yarn tail ends on the wrong side of your fabric with a blunt tapestry needle. Draw the yarn through at least 5cm (2in) of stitches and then weave it back in the opposite direction for 2.5cm (1in) to prevent the end from working loose. Make sure to weave through the loops of your stitches and not into the yarn itself.

Note: Try weaving in your yarn ends as you work, especially on projects with lots of colour changes. It will make finishing your project much easier.

seams

A beautiful crochet fabric can easily be ruined by careless sewing up. Practise on a spare piece of fabric if you are unsure of the method suggested before starting the garment. There are several ways to join seams and more than one method can be used in a project. Decide what you want to achieve. If you don't want the seam to be noticed, then mattress stitch (also called ladder stitch) is a good choice.

MATTRESS STITCH SEAM

The mattress stitch seam is an invisible seam, and it is used to sew crocheted fabrics together. Unlike a crocheted seam, it has no bulk, and it is used mostly in garment construction.

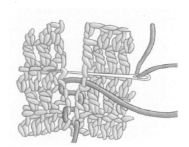

Place the crocheted pieces on a flat surface with the right sides facing up. Take time to make sure the stitches are aligned. Thread the needle through the post of the bottom right stitch, cross over to the corresponding left stitch, and at the same time draw the yarn through the post of the stitch. Continue working back and forth through the posts of the stitches. Gently tighten the seam while you work, but don't make it too tight.

finishing your work

Finishing your work properly is often essential to the longevity and visual appeal of your crochet.

To fasten off your work, simply pull the loop that is on the hook nice and loose, and pass the working yarn through the loop, pulling tightly to make a neat knot. Fastening off in this way ensures an invisible join. Cut off the working yarn, leaving a tail of around 7.5cm (3in) long.

To make the yarn ends disappear, you'll need to weave them into the work. Thread your darning needle, and pass the needle through the back of the stitches on the wrong side of the work, so you cannot see the weave from the front. Pass through as many stitches as you like to ensure an invisible end. Cut yarn if necessary.

blocking and pressing

Blocking your work is the act of shaping it, and it's worth doing this to make the most of your work. The majority of projects in this book can, and should, be blocked. It doesn't take long and really ensures that the shape and construction of the work is shown how it should be. Some shapes and fibres can simply be pulled into shape, but other shapes will benefit from blocking – particularly shaped blocks or those with curved edges (usually when a block is crocheted in double crochet).

For light blocking, lay the work out to its true shape and pin it. You can pin it to a folded towel or an ironing board. Place a damp cloth over the work and press lightly with a cool iron. Check the yarn label for care advice — some acrylic yarns should not be ironed.

For heavy blocking, usually with natural fibres, lay the work out and pin it. Cover with a damp cloth and steam press gently. Leave the work somewhere warm until totally dry. Remove the pins.

joining blocks

Joining blocks together is a great way of making projects, elevating crochet to much more than just the sum of its parts. The easiest way of joining blocks together is to use matching yarn and a darning needle.

First, lay out the blocks and decide which order they will go in. If you can, leave them on the floor or table in this order so that you can keep track. Or take a photograph to refer back to if you're joining lots of blocks together. Work in rows, joining the top row together block by block. Once all the horizontal rows are joined together, you can join the vertical rows.

essential hints and tips

When working the stitches, you typically work each stitch into the top of the stitches on the row below. If you look at the crochet from above, you'll see a series of 'V's that look like the chain. Insert the hook just under the 'V', which will be working into the top 2 loops of the stitch.

When working with back and forth patterns, you'll need to turn the work at the end of a row. Flip your crochet from left to right 180 degrees, so that the hook is now on the right-hand side of the row.

Working into just the front loop or just the back loop of the stitch will give you a ribbed, ridged effect, and the crocheted item will not lie flat.

There is often a right side and wrong side in crochet. They look different, but can be equally attractive. When working with back and forth patterns, alternate rows will be worked with the right side facing. In most patterns worked in the round, you'll be crocheting with the right side facing.

When working in rounds, you'll usually (though not always) begin with a foundation chain. Join the chain into a loop by inserting the hook into the very first chain made, YRH, then pull this loop through the yarn on the hook. This is slip stitching the chain together to form a loop. You will finish each round in the same way, inserting the hook into the first stitch worked, and drawing the yarn through the loop on the hook to slip stitch the edges together.

Changing colour is usually done at the end of the row, but can also be done mid-row. The technique is the same. Let the working yarn fall behind the work. Wrap the new colour around your hand, and make a loop through the loop on the hook. Pull the tail of the old colour tight. You now have the new colour as your working yarn.

To save time if weaving in ends when you're working in colour, work in the ends as you go. When you change colour, cut your tail ends the same length, then hold them along the top of the previous row. When you work the next row, the stitches will capture the ends and conceal them.

crochet diagrams

Most crochet patterns are written out in words but will often include a chart or graph. Charts use symbols to represent each stitch, allowing you to see at a glance how the fabric is constructed. They are read slightly differently depending on whether the fabric is worked row by row or in the round.

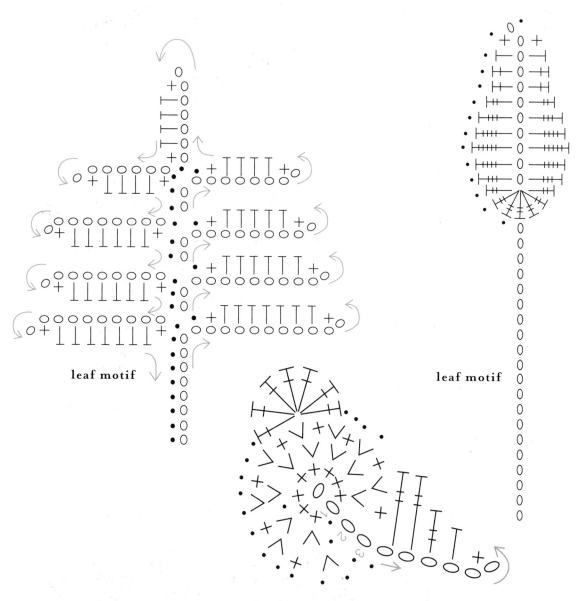

leaf motif

leaf motif

birdie (work in reverse for underside)

ROW BY ROW

▦ This type of chart is read from the bottom up

▦ Right side rows are worked from right to left, wrong side rows are read from left to right

▦ A row number shows where the row begins and can also be accompanied by an arrow showing the direction you are reading the chart

▦ You alternate from right side to wrong side on each row.

IN THE ROUND

▦ This type of chart is read from the centre out, working in an anticlockwise direction

▦ You are always working with the right side facing, unless the pattern instructs you otherwise

▦ It can be helpful to place a marker at the beginning of each round

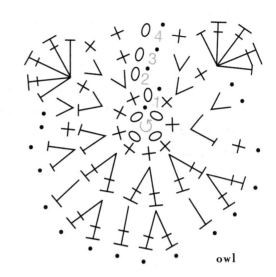

owl

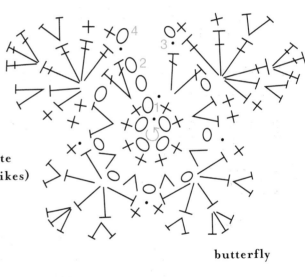

butterfly

snowflake (alternate large and small spikes)

napkin ring

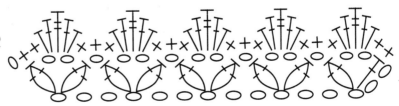

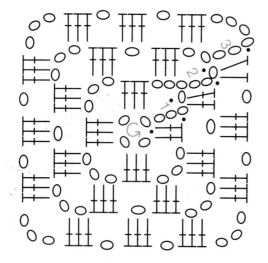

slip cover

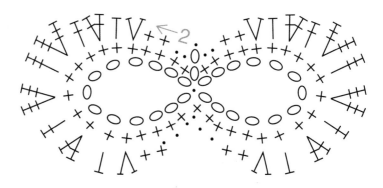

hair bow loop

1

hair bow tail

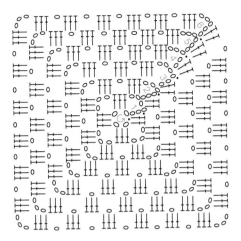

table runner

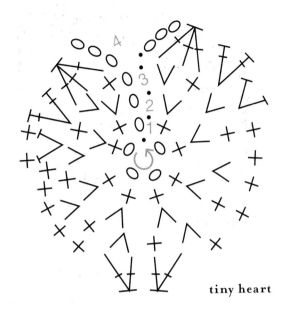

tiny heart

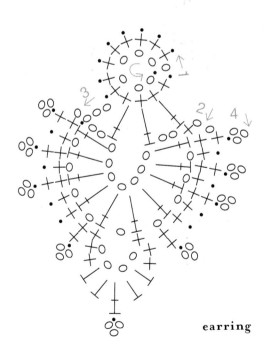

earring

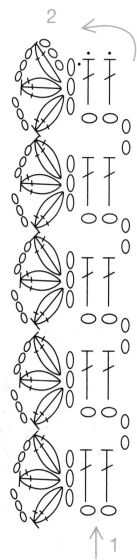

2

1

lace necklace

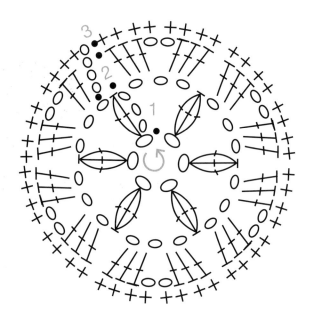

3

2

1

hexagon motif purse

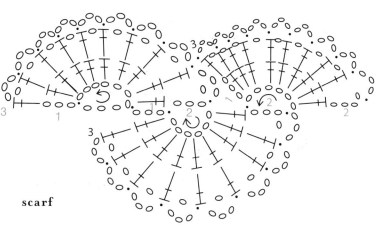

scarf

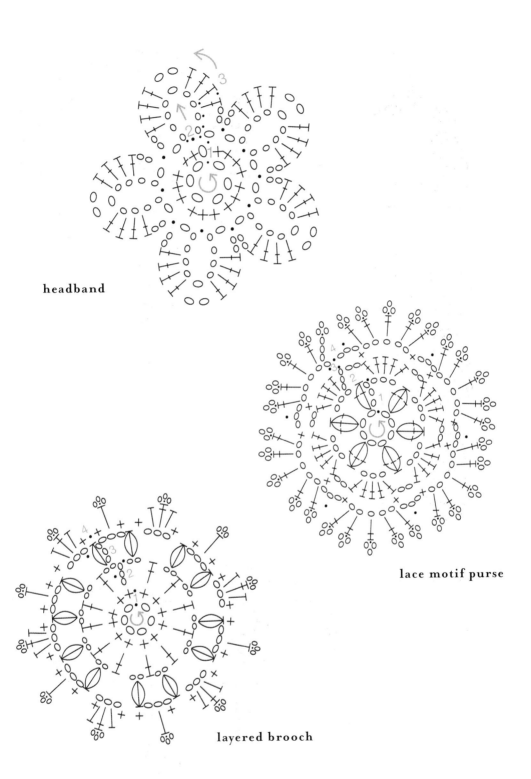

headband

lace motif purse

layered brooch

index

Page numbers in **bold** type refer to diagrams; numbers in *italic type* refer to photographs.

acknowledgements

Carol Meldrum: I would like to thank everybody for their help and support creating this fantastic book. Rowan and Coats Crafts UK for supplying the lovely materials used throughout the projects. My ever so patient and loving partner Andy Daly for supplying me with constant care and attention throughout. Thank you — I couldn't have done this without you all!

Quintet Publishing would also like to thank:
Nguyen Le for pattern testing each project and Mandy Webster for the photography location.